Latin Music
Through the Ages

Latin Music
Through the Ages

Cynthia Kaldis

Bolchazy - Carducci Publishers

General Editor: Georgine Cooper
Cover and Book Design: Sharyn Yulish-Lusty

© Copyright 1991
Cynthia Kaldis

Published by
Bolchazy-Carducci Publishers, Inc.
1000 Brown Street, #101
Wauconda, Illinois 60084 USA

ISBN: 0-86516-242-5

Printed in the United States of America
1999 Corrected Reprint

Library of Congress Cataloging-in-Publication Data

Kaldis, Cynthia 1933-
　　Latin music through the ages / Cynthia Kaldis.
　　　　p.　　cm.
　　Includes poetical works in Latin with English translation.
　　Includes bibliographical references.
　　ISBN 0-86516-242-5　$15.00
　　1. Sacred vocal music — Texts — History and criticism.
　　2. Vocal music — Texts — History and criticism. 3. Sacred
　　vocal music — Texts. 4. Vocal music — Texts. 5. Latin poetry
　　— Translations into English. I. Title
　　ML1400.K34 1991
　　782.2'026'8 — dc20　　　　　　　　　　　　　91-39530
　　　　　　　　　　　　　　　　　　　　　　　　　　　　CIP
　　　　　　　　　　　　　　　　　　　　　　　　　　　　MN

To Nick,
my Purdue connection.

TABLE OF CONTENTS

PREFACE

During my years of teaching high school Latin, each Christmas season I have experienced a sense of disappointment that I could not provide a musical experience for my students. We had, of course, our song sheets for which I was an enthusiastic, though untalented, song leader. When we came to *Adeste Fideles*, a genuine Latin carol, the students sensed that there was something special, but they really preferred "Deck the Halls" because even the most inept student could manage the "fa la la."

The other feeling of disappointment was more nebulous. When I was so fortunate as to attend a concert which included some Latin music, or, better yet, if the program was all Latin, perhaps a Requiem, I came away from the concert wanting to share with my students some of my emotions when I heard the beautiful Latin words and the equally beautiful music which they had inspired. There is, I thought, another dimension to Latin, one which will perhaps intersect a student's life in his or her adult years, as much as mythology, derivatives, or remembered bits of Roman life and history. From this notion about Latin music as a relatively untapped source of enrichment for the classroom, this project has developed.

It is my good fortune to live in a university town, and through several summers I spent my days in the Music Library of Ohio University where I soon came to the realization that I knew almost nothing about Latin music. But the glory of a library is that one book leads to another, certain names keep turning up in bibliographies, and gradually the *terra incognita* begins to take on some identifiable features. At times I became lost in wonder among the incomparably moving hymns of the early church. Then came the student songs of the Middle Ages, listening again to the *Carmina Burana* with Judith Sebasta's excellent text as a guide, or reading Helen Waddell's superb poetic translations. There were other discoveries as well, about the history of carols, medieval mystery plays, and the seemingly incomprehensible development of the Roman Catholic liturgy.

While I was immersing myself in the search for appropriate Latin texts, I was also trying to find a group which would undertake the performance of the music. Several trial collaborations with university musicians seemed to hold the answer, but the reality was otherwise. Student choral groups have performance schedules built into their academic year; they have limited rehearsal time and even more limited budgets for buying music and renting a recording studio. My son, who was studying at Purdue University, mentioned to me several times that one of his English professors had a group of musicians who liked to do "old music" and that I should talk with him about my project. It was the best phone call I ever made. Dr. Clayton Lein did indeed have a group, the Lafayette Chamber Singers, and they did specialize in "old music." Phrased more appropriately, the Singers are a non-profit organization dedicated to the performance of seldom heard music from earlier periods.

The collaboration with Clayton Lein has been fortuitous for the final form of this project, *Latin Music Through the Ages*. His fine musician's ear, expertise in performance, and sense of audience were what was needed. To my list of possible texts, he added his knowledge of Renaissance music and performance repertoire, always reminding me that the recording had to stand on its own as a musical production and, as such, should have variety of sound and style in its exploration of the many facets of Latin music over the centuries.

In the Introduction I have attempted a general background of the development of sacred and secular Latin verse forms. The Bibliography provides ample sources for further reading. Some information seemed in order on the Latin pronunciation used by musicians. For each selection of the recording I have compiled a brief biography of the author of the text and general information about the historical setting of the original verse. The composers also are deserving of biographical remarks: many are unfamiliar names to us non-musicians, and some, like the Renaissance composer Jacob Handl, have a fascinating story to tell. The Latin texts are printed in their entirety wherever possible, and the English translations are drawn from many published sources, although a few are my own.

Much of the music on the recording comes, of course, from the rituals of the Roman Catholic Church, since Latin was the language of the Catholic Church until the tremendous changes brought about by Vatican II in the sixties. For centuries, in the Western world, Latin was the language of religious thought and emotion; the Christian writer, with few exceptions, used Latin. For an even longer period, when a composer searched for a text to set to music, he almost always dipped into that same great linguistic treasury. For all those centuries Latin served the artist, whether writer or musician, and this is the fact to be stressed. The language had a versatility, an adaptability, a poetic beauty that I have come to appreciate much more as a result of the present undertaking. My hope is that other Latin teachers will share in the historical wonder of this language, which gave a voice to Hildegard of Bingen in the twelfth century, as well as to Pablo Casals in the twentieth, when he composed the moving choral lamentation *O vos omnes*. The language is Latin, it is catholic, and it is universal.

The inclusion of six selections on the recording by twentieth century composers, which I can attribute primarily to Clayton Lein's influence, has been musically and intellectually significant. The modern compositions give a solidity, I believe, to the project as a sampling of Latin choral music across the centuries. At the same time I find this intellectually unsettling because it has forced me to consider that Duruflé, Messiaen and the others may be the final chapter of Latin sacred choral music.

Those of us who have studied Latin as a classical language have tough hides when it comes to the barbs about Latin being a "dead" language. Most Latin teachers try to deal with Latin's demise with good humor, wisdom, and always with a vigorous counterattack. Somehow, I suspect, in our private thoughts, we long derived comfort from the thought that Latin was being kept "alive" within the Roman Catholic tradition. If a non-Catholic classicist silently mourns the loss of this liturgical life line, I wonder how the Roman Catholic Church is coping with the loss of its historic linguistic oneness.

Church Music Transgressed by Francis P. Schmitt, a Capuchin musician, speaks to the matter of the disappearance of the Latin Mass and its effect on the music of the Church. Father Schmitt refers to the liturgical reform of Vatican II as a revolution, not a reform. As in any revolution, there is chaos, lack of respect for authority, loss of standards of excellence, and the disregard for logic. Schmitt draws a Hegelian parallel of thesis, antithesis and synthesis. "The antithetic period has been, and still is, so devastating and pervasive that I do not expect any of us to be around for the synthesis when and if it comes."

The problem for the Church is that its liturgical music evolved from simple plainchant to complex harmonies along with an evolving Latin language, but the two were always an artistic whole: sacred music is also art. To superimpose modern vernacular languages on traditional melodies does not work. New music will be required to complete the new liturgy, and it will take years for the creative process to fulfill such a high calling. In the meantime, a great deal of inferior music will be heard. Father Schmitt observes:

> The crux of the matter was the vernacular, and there the chant caught it from both left and right. Both insisted that with the passing of Latin, Gregorian chant too would be passé. The left had always held the simplistic theory that somehow the problem of Church music was a linguistic not a musical one, and that, given the vernacular, song — the know-how and the desire for it — would appear in the land. The right insisted that Gregorian be saved in its Latin home or there would be none. And shortly there was none.

In the meantime there is still the concert hall where Latin will continue to be sung and to be heard in myriad settings, many of which will reach wider audiences through the electronic media. It is hard to imagine a day when Beethoven's *Missa Solemnis* or Verdi's *Requiem* would play to anything less than full capacity. Those who love the ancient tongue can find comfort that its enduring richness will survive, not only in the great classical authors, but also in the vast and varied corpus of Latin choral music.

In this project I have received constant encouragement from John Dutra, director of the Teaching Materials and Resource Center of the American Classical League at Miami University, Oxford, Ohio. I have been assisted by Ira Zook, Richard Wetzel and Reginald Fink of the music faculty at Ohio University, and by Peter Gano, musicologist at Ohio State University. Paul Murphy, professor emeritus of classical languages at Ohio University, has been most generous with his learned assistance. I was fortunate to have an interview with Richard Hoppin, author of *Medieval Music*, and profited from his suggestions. Deep gratitude goes to the Martha Holden Jennings Foundation for its financial support, especially for having seen some worth in the project in its early stages, and to my employer, Alexander Local School District, for its institutional support. The final manuscript was immeasurably enhanced by the artistic and editorial expertise of Elizabeth Kortlander. Finally, I am mindful of the debt I owe to Clayton Lein and the Lafayette Chamber Singers for creating music where there were only words. My husband Bill thought all along that I could do this; I did not want to let him down.

Cynthia Kaldis
Athens, Ohio

August, 1991

INTRODUCTION

*L*atin Music Through the Ages can be appreciated solely for the beauty and variety of the musical forms, spanning, as they do, centuries of musical history. Since many will also wish to focus on the Latin texts which are the inspiration of the choral settings, the introductory material offers some background reading on the development of Latin sacred and secular verse in the Middle Ages. A subject so complex in terms both of history and of language is not easily condensed. By the inclusion of a selected bibliography, the reader is offered several excellent sources for a more thorough exploration of later Latin poetry. Those who are already knowledgeable about Latin hymnology and medieval profane verse will recognize that the introduction is a cursory treatment. Those who have a background in the classical Latin authors, however, may find that these verses arouse their curiosity to do further reading and listening, so that the work of the medieval poets will reaffirm their appreciation of Latin's enduring beauty.

Sacred Verse

There is no bridge that can span the ancient pagan Roman world and the world of the early Christian church; for there is no gap separating the two co-existing worlds which shared time, space, language, culture, and institutions. The Latin fathers of the Church, even those who wrote most emphatically against paganism, had been trained in classical schools of grammar, which meant that they had studied the great works of Greek and Roman literature. Even that most venerated of church fathers, St. Augustine, in his *Confessions* wrote that Vergil had been for him, since boyhood, the prince of poets, whose tale of poor Dido had brought tears to his eyes. The medievalist F. J. E. Raby concludes that there were scarcely any early Christian poets who did not owe their training to the classical grammarians and rhetoricians.

By the fourth century there are identifiable Christian authors who wrote poetry neither for the emperor nor for literate and cultured friends, but for the glorification of their faith. First among those who wrote Latin sacred verse was Hilary, Bishop of Poitiers (c. 310-366), who made use of hymns in celebration of the Trinity to refute the powerful fourth century Arian heresy. Arianism had spread so rapidly among early Christians that the Emperor Constantine summoned the first general council of the church at Nicaea in 325 to counteract the growing heresy, which denied the divinity of Christ and the Holy Spirit. Within this conflict between the Arians and the adherents of the orthodox trinitarian doctrine, hymn writing emerged. The priest Arius of Alexandria (280-336), like the earlier Syrian Gnostic heretics, capitalized on the popular taste for secular melodies, among them some lewd lyrics of Greek origin; he took the melodies, but changed the words in order to create dogmatic hymns which promoted Arian beliefs. St. Hilary, in a musical counterattack, wrote hymns, of which three have survived, celebrating the orthodox trinitarian view.

St. Ambrose (340-397), also from Gaul, is generally acknowledged as the originator of the Latin hymn in the form still familiar to

Albrecht Dürer (1471-1528), *St. Ambrose*, woodcut. Courtesy of A.L. Van Gendt B.V., Amsterdam.

us: a uniform series of metrical stanzas for congregational singing. Again, Arianism had a role, for Ambrose, who had been appointed Bishop of Milan, was moved to compose his religious songs in response to the persecution of his congregation by the Empress Justina, a follower of Arianism. Marie Pierik, in her work *The Song of the Church,* quotes Ambrose, who felt the need to justify his hymns as an antidote to heresy. "Moreover, they assert that the people have been beguiled by the strains of my hymns. I deny not this either. It is a lofty strain, than which nothing is more powerful." The hymns of Ambrose represent the beginning of Latin Christian poetry, and the power of the lyrics, as Ambrose himself proclaimed, touched the hearts of worshippers. St. Augustine felt such raptures at hearing Ambrose's hymns that he wept tears of gladness. So influential was Ambrose that many hymns of this early period of unknown or uncertain authorship are referred to simply as Ambrosian.

Immediately following Ambrose came another great figure in the early history of the Latin hymn, Prudentius of Spain (348-c. 413), a Spanish magistrate rather than a cleric, who had received his appointment from the Emperor Theodosius I. Prudentius was a true poet who produced literary poems, not hymns, some of which were very soon incorporated as song into the liturgy. In *Hymns and the Christian Myth*, Lionel Adey selects Prudentius' hymn *Corde natus ex parentis* as "the earliest and most complete account still in use of the Christian myth, that enfolds history." Adey quotes this stanza of the hymn with a 1905 translation by R. F. Davis:

Corde natus ex parentis	Of the Father's heart begotten,
ante mundi exordium	ere the world from chaos rose,
A et O cognominatus,	he is Alpha: from that Fountain
ipse fons et clausula	all that is and hath been flows;
Omnium quae sunt, fuerunt,	He is Omega, of all things
quaeque post futura sunt	yet to come the mystic close,
saeculorum saeculis.	evermore and evermore.

Prudentius witnessed the last gasps of paganism under Julian the Apostate, but he saw, in Adey's words, "... in the splendid new basilicas evidence not of the decay but of the renewal of Rome through the triumph of the true faith over the pagan mystery cults."

In these earliest centuries of sacred Latin verse, the liturgy itself was in its formative period. Official Rome was openly hostile to the new Christian sect, imperial Rome was faced with barbarian invasions, the infant church was already plagued with heresies, and paganism, although moribund, was not yet totally gone from the scene. Yet in such times both Ambrose and Prudentius found in their faith the inspiration to write hymns to uplift the assembled believers, for the verse form which they created made these hymns accessible to Christian congregations.

Julian Notary (active c. 1500), *Expositio sequentiarum*, woodcut. Courtesy of Oxford University Press.

From the fifth to the eighth centuries hymn sources are scanty and authorship seldom known. One name, however, stands forth, Venantius Fortunatus (c 530–600), whose two great masterpieces, *Pange lingua* and *Vexilla regis prodeunt*, were written in celebration of the Holy Cross. The latter hymn was composed by Fortunatus on the occasion of a relic of the cross being presented to the Abbey of the True Cross at Poitiers where Fortunatus presided as bishop. Both hymns have been described as "martial," for the imagery is that of Christ triumphant, continuing the image of the cross as a sign of victory, as it had appeared to the Emperor Constantine. With

Catholicism triumphant in the Roman world, the transition to the medieval age was underway, and with the appearance of the Vulgate Bible of St. Jerome, Latin was secure as the dominant language of the Western world.

Although these early centuries produced great innovators of Christian Latin verse, some of which has come down to us, we know little about the music to which the verse was sung as hymns. The speculation about the form of the music is partially resolved by acknowledging that there were certain musical forms with which these early Christians were familiar, and hymn singing assuredly drew on these forms. They were the music of the Jewish worship service, Greek music, and contemporary folk music.

The link between existing Jewish synagogue practice and early Christian worship is often suggested as the origin of hymn singing. The medievalist Raby emphasizes this when he states that "the Psalms of David became the hymn-book of the Church... and the Jewish psalm was the model of the earliest Christian hymns." In the Hebrew musical tradition psalm singing was not only a form of worship but also a form of religious instruction, both of which are attributes of hymn singing as well. Aside from psalmody, there were hymns whose lyrics could be either direct quotes from the Scriptures or liberal paraphrases of sacred texts. The musical linkage between the synagogue and the primitive church has received critical scrutiny from J. A. Smith in an article in *Music and Letters.* Smith's thesis is that there is no absolute documentation for singing in the synagogue service prior to the second century. The only synagogue practice which came near to singing was the cantillation of scripture, a sort of rhythmical reading with special attention to intonation. Smith posits that the Jewish influence came, instead, through private religious and domestic assemblies for Passover, weddings or funerals, and the like, or intimate family gatherings for the religious instruction of children; for all such occasions singing can be documented. The private religious assemblies of the early Christians, held in the homes of the faithful, had much in common with the extra-synagogue Jewish gatherings, notably in the sharing of a common meal. In this context songs of praise, that is hymns, are mentioned in the New Testament and elsewhere. Smith concludes:

> The similarities in the nature of the singing at Jewish private religious assemblies and early Christian assemblies, taken in conjunction with the resemblances between the circumstances of such assemblies and viewed in the light of the Jewish background of Christianity, provide strong grounds for regarding the private religious assemblies as the specific area of Jewish religious life from which Christian singing stemmed.

Another musical influence on the early Christians of the Near East was the extant Greek musical tradition. In classical times the Greeks had subjected music to its first scientific study, identifying various musical modes, each with a musical scale. In addition to the scale, the Greeks had invented a form of musical notation; unfortunately, few examples have survived. There is literary evidence, to be sure, of musical performances and of a high regard in the Greco-Roman world for talented musicians, but

Anton Woensam (after 1500-1541), *Concert,* woodcut. Courtesy of Hacker Art Books, Inc.

the sounds of the music are virtually unknown. That also holds true for the popular folk music which was another component of the musical environment of the early church.

Scholars agree that the music of the Latin church had its beginnings in the East, but that the gradual shift of the focus of Christian authority to Rome brought this Eastern music into a different liturgical and linguistic context. The rudimentary prayer meetings of the early Christians followed the Jewish practice of responsive singing of the psalms in which the cantor, being the experienced vocalist, could elaborate his chant with increasingly complex modulations. The congregation, for its part, kept to a simpler form of singing. The Mass itself, in its formative stages, was open to diversity among the scattered congregations, although it kept to its basic liturgical structure. With the adoption of Latin as the language of the liturgy, a gradual process of the third and fourth centuries, the chants, the readings and the responses of the Church became more and more formalized. In fact, Hoppin notes, "The strict regulation of every detail in the services for the entire year, perhaps an expression of the Roman genius for organization, has remained characteristic of the Roman liturgy almost to the present time." Hoppin attributes the development of much of medieval music to the desire of Christian congregations to adapt the Mass to their own particular preferences, especially by the embellishment of the music.

As the Mass became more rigidly formal, the prayer services of monastic life preserved much of the character of the early Christian gatherings, and it was to the worship of the Offices that St. Ambrose added hymn singing. Monastic life, in its turn, was also subjected to a more formal structure when the Rule of St. Benedict was imposed in the sixth century.

At the end of the sixth century the chief figure in the development of the Roman liturgy and its music ascended the papal throne, Gregory I (590-640). For centuries Pope Gregory was regarded as the originator of the chant style used in the Roman Church: plainsong, or *cantus firmus* (smooth, level song). In fact, he was pictured in manuscripts receiving his inspiration for the chant from the Holy Spirit, in the form of a dove. The revival of studies in liturgical history has brought forth new interpretations on the origin of the chant, in no way as simple as the tradition of Gregory's divine inspiration.

Gregory's achievements as the supreme pontiff were remarkable in every sense, and he is credited with the establishment of the universal authority of the Church of Rome. As a corollary to that authority, Gregory imposed a Roman standard on both the liturgy and the chant. Although pious tradition, mentioned above, gave Gregory credit for composing the chants, the clearer interpretation of his role was that he standardized the Mass chants in a form called the *Antiphonarium Gregorianum*. His concern for music can be seen, as well, in the encouragement he gave to the *schola cantorum* (school of singers), whose trained

The Singing Lesson, woodcut, from *Spiegel des menschlichen Lebens,* Augsburg, c. 1475. Courtesy of Constable & Co., Ltd.

singers spread the Gregorian chant model throughout the Latin West.

Gregory was astute in promoting and regulating the use of music in the Mass, for this most important ritual of the Church had, in its formative stages, been conceived as a sacred drama. The altar ceremonies, whether performed by Pope, bishop, or priest, were reinforced by the chanting of the clergy and the musical responses of the choir and congregation, creating a dramatic unity of words and music. Through the evolution from unisonous chant to the modern use of polyphonic choral music with instrumental accompaniment, this union of words and music has remained a central feature of Catholic religious ceremony.

Gregory's standardization of liturgical music was the precursor of a great revival of Latin hymnody under the Carolingian rulers from 750 to 900 A. D., a period of varied European contacts, with clerics and government officials traveling throughout the Frankish Empire. During the reign of Charlemagne there were, in addition, clear traces of Byzantine influences on Western liturgical music, and the emperor was known to have admired the splendor of the Eastern Christian rites.

This same Carolingian period was a time of retreat for the Latin language, however, as it became less in use by anyone other than the clergy. Latin hymns may have graced the gatherings of early medieval Christians, but the common Christian folk of Europe had little knowledge of hymnology. The composition and preservation of hymns can be attributed solely to their introduction into monastic life, where the hymn was associated primarily with the monastic canonical hours, and, to a much lesser extent, with congregational singing. Monastic practice developed a daily *cursus* of services, seven in number, for which increasing numbers and varieties hymns were employed.

During the late Carolingian period, as the hymn moved from the monastery to a new position of importance in the liturgy of the Mass, other new musical developments appeared. Although the form of the Mass itself had been standardized, the liturgy was flexible in the sense that it allowed for musical and textual additions to the various parts of the Mass. One of these textual additions was the trope, which could be either prose or poetry, and was used to explain or amplify the meaning of a particular liturgical passage. Another was the sequence, which eventually came to be used in much the same way as the hymn. The origin of the sequence, both in its musical and in its literary form, is a complex matter and the subject of some scholarly debate. In simple terms, the sequence is an outgrowth of the musical practice of prolonging the final syllable of the *Alleluia* in the Mass. As the final -a was elaborated into longer musical phrases, it became necessary to divide the extended phrases for the sake of breathing. The next step was the addition of a text written below the musical notation of the sequence; this was referred to as a *prosa*, an abbreviated form of *Pro s[equenti]a*. Gradually the texts, each with its own tune, evolved into verse form; the verse form became more and more poetical, made greater use of rhyme, and culminated in some of the loveliest lyrics of medieval poetry. What had begun as a musical ornamentation of the Mass, gradually took on an independent poetic form, using as themes, among others, the great seasons of the church year and the feasts of the saints.

Those sequences most frequently cited for the beauty of their lyrics are *Veni Sancte Spiritus* (Come, Holy Spirit), written in the twelfth century for the feast of Pentecost; *Dies Irae* (Day of Wrath), composed by Thomas of Celano (d. c. 1255), whose dramatic verses can be heard in Verdi's *Requiem*; the *Stabat Mater*, written by the Franciscan Jacopone da Todi (d. 1306), whose passionate words of sorrow move the listener, whether in the polyphonic setting of Palestrina, or in the original simple chant form; and *Jesu, dulcis memoria*, a long poem dubiously ascribed to St. Bernard of Clairvaux (d. 1153), which is found in many modern hymn collections as "Jesu, the Very Thought of Thee."

The sources for medieval chants, hymns, and sequences are found in the numerous liturgical chant books of European cathedrals and monasteries, as well as in the manuscript collections of libraries throughout the Western world. In the later Middle Ages, liturgists, working under monastic or episcopal authority, examined old psalters and other compilations of hymns, preserving some, and, unfortunately, discarding others of the sacred texts. The breviary was such an assemblage. One, which was produced in Salisbury, England, called the *Sarum Rite*, contained 119 hymns and 101 sequences.

The most popular collection of devotions and hymns was the Book of

Hours which was widely used in western Europe from the mid-thirteenth century into the Renaissance. Although most Books of Hours were in Latin, vernacular editions also exist; in the Netherlands in particular, vernacular Books predominated by up to ninety percent. The basic text of the Book of Hours consisted of eight services which could be recited at different times of the day, known collectively as the Little Office of the Blessed Virgin Mary. The Little Office was intended for the laity who wished to imitate, in the secular world, the daily recital of the Offices as practiced by the clergy. A Book of Hours commonly included a church calendar and other readings and prayers appropriate for specific occasions, as well as devotional hymns. Although Books of Hours are a source of hymns, they are chiefly prized for the beauty of their illustrations.

Old English engraving.
Courtesy of Dick Sutphen Studio.

It should be noted that corresponding to the widespread practice of private devotions, as exemplified in the Books of Hours, is the trend toward less formal music. In *Style and Symbol* Andrew Hughes remarks that from the twelfth century the influence of the monastic setting for liturgical chanting begins to wane, and music for informal devotions was more and more in demand. Hughes gives the Franciscans an important role in the introduction of popular song as a musical setting for the church liturgy. The itinerant friars of the Franciscan order were exposed to the informal music of daily life, and they brought these folk traditions into the liturgical setting, loosening some of the complex traditions of ritual music associated with the monastic choirs.

From the popularity of the Books of Hours it is evident that the Latin hymns of the late medieval period were widely known in the Christian West. Their influence on secular and religious verse forms is pervasive, for medieval poets, writing in the vernacular languages, often found their inspiration, if not their poetic model, in the Latin hymns. English poets of the thirteenth, fourteenth, and fifteenth centuries translated, adapted, and imitated Latin models. Since the hymns of the medieval period occupy this pivotal position between classical Latin and the later vernacular poetry of Europe, Raby has made this observation:

> The whole literary imagination of the West was to be fed on the sonorous sentences of the Latin Bible, and Christian poetry, though true so long to its learned traditions, could not escape the spell or fail to learn the new language... It is the music of a new world, for out of it appeared at last, when its religious mission had been fulfilled, the romantic poetry of the modern world.

The subject matter of hymns was a vast and ever-expanding field from which the hymnist could draw inspiration. Not only were theology and Biblical passages used as hymn topics, but the veneration of saints, the teaching of moral precepts, and historical events served as well. From such diversity of subject matter the hymnists were able to experiment with new imagery and poetic language, much of which found its way into secular poetry.

At the same time, the full creative scope of hymn writing drew on its classical and pagan antecedents, of which Joseph Szövérffy presents several interesting examples in his work *A Concise History of Medieval Hymnody*. Common classical allusions are the identification of God with Jupiter, the devil with Pluto, and the Virgin Mary with, variously, Proserpina, Minerva, Diana, and even Venus. In early French hymns and sequences the Muses are invoked. One particular French saint, Martial,

Bishop of Limoges (c. 250 A.D.), was the subject of several legends, among them that he was actually an apostle of Christ's own lifetime. In eleventh century France the cult of St. Martial flourished. The following hymn names all nine of the Muses, who sing with lyres and flutes in praise of Martial, the patriarch and disciple of the Lord:

> *Intensis modulis pulchris fidibus variatis*
> *Calliope, Thalia, Clio, Melpomene, Musae*
> *Euterpe, soror Uraniaque canant modulando,*
> *Sic Erato cum Terpsichore, Polyhymnia dulcis*
> *Tibicinumque chorus, cantorum turma resultent*
> *Martialem Domini patriarcham discipulumque...*

> [With lyre strings tuned to varying and beautiful rhythms
> The Muses, Calliope, Thalia, Clio, Melpomene,
> Euterpe and Urania, her sister, sing in measure;
> So, too, Erato with Terpsichore, sweet Polyhymnia
> And the chorus of pipers, the throng of singers, all praise
> Martial, the patriarch and disciple of the Lord. . . .]

There are, in addition, references to the Greek philosophers Plato and Aristotle, whose wisdom, says one poet, is surpassed by that of St. Catherine, who sought to convert the Emperor Maximinus from his idolatry. The Emperor, unable himself to refute her arguments, sent for the pagan philosophers, who were, in turn, confounded by her wise discourse. In this sequence of St. Catherine, her eloquence has outshone that of Cicero and Demosthenes, made the wise appear as fools, and won the homage of no less a personage than Vergil himself.

> *Tullianae rivos*
>   *eloquentiae,*
> *Torrentem Demosthenis*
>   *superat facundia.*

> *Nam Platonis,*
>   *Aristotelis dogmata*
> *In sui cordis gerebat*
>   *haec penetralibus;*

Latentis naturae
> peritos rerum

Sapientia sui
> in stuporem convertit.

Mantuanus
> ille Maro, vatum princeps

Se iudice carminibus
> vinctum se dicebat.

[Her facile speech surpasses the streams of Tullian eloquence,
the torrent of Demosthenes.
For she carries the teachings of Plato and of Aristotle
in the recesses of her heart.
The wisdom of her secret nature confounds
those clever in worldly affairs.
Maro the Mantuan, prince of poets, by his own judgment
proclaims himself captivated by her songs.]

Szövérffy notes, as well, that the medieval hymnists on various occasions
adapted Vergil's fourth Eclogue, which contained the so-called Messianic
prophecy, to their Christian themes.

These brief observations about the rise of chant, hymn, and sequence
barely touch the many musical terms associated with sacred Latin music
and verse, terms which are both specialized and technical. Because of the
Christmas music on the recording, the term "carol" deserves some particular attention, especially since, having its origins in the medieval period, the
carol represents another aspect of Latin music of the Middle Ages.

In the popular mind a carol is associated with the Christmas season,
which is reflected in the 1911 *Encyclopaedia Britannica*'s definition "A
hymn of praise, especially such as is sung at Christmas in the open air."
Other definitions stress, rather than its seasonal usage, its association with
the dance, particularly the dance-songs of the French and English courts.
There is, furthermore, in the elaboration of the origins of the carol, a
suggestion that the carol was derived, in part, from a processional hymn,
or *conductus*, sung before the reading of the Gospel. Richard Leighton
Greene has produced an extensive study in *The Early English Carols*, and
his definition, focusing on the carol as it was employed in the sixteenth

century, is "A song on any subject, composed of uniform stanzas and provided with a burden." The burden is a chorus, or refrain, which the choir sings before the opening stanza and repeats after each stanza.

An examination of the carol, especially in its early stages of development, leads once again to the influence of Latin. This popular genre made widespread use of macaronic verse, that is verse with a mixture of languages. In many cases Latin quotations were blended into the vernacular, a widespread practice in the sacred and secular music of England and Europe during the medieval and Renaissance periods. Greene has collected 502 carols, of which 210 contain Latin lines or phrases.

In the macaronic verse of England the interworking of English and Latin takes a number of different forms. In some, the stanza consists of alternating lines of English and Latin:

> Vpon a nyght an aungell bright
> > Pastoribus apparuit,
> And shone right thrugh Goddes myght
> > Lux magna illis claruit.
> > > For loue of vu (Scripture seith thus)
> > > Nunc natus est Altissimus

Other carols combined an English stanza with a Latin *cauda*, or tail-rhyme, as in this carol for the Epiphany:

> Ther ys a blossom sprong of a thorn
> To saue mankynd, that was forlorne,
> As the profettes sayd beforne;
> > Deo Patri sit gloria.

In addition, Latin is found in the burden of many carols as in this song to the Virgin:

> Nowell, nowell, nowell, nowell
> Myssus est virginem angelus Gabriell.

While some of the Latin lyrics in the macaronic carols show originality of authorship, the usual case is for bits of familiar Latin to be employed. Sometimes the quotes are merely clichés from common religious utterances, rather like, "God bless us all!" At other times the Latin lines are taken from church ritual, especially from the best known medieval hymns, such as this burden which contains a line from Fortunatus' great Passiontide hymn:

> Now synge we, as we were wont:
> "Uexilla Regis prodeunt."

The beloved Latin Christmas carol, *Adeste Fideles*, is a later product, dating from the eighteenth century. Both the words and the music date to a 1743 manuscript, whose author is identified as John Francis Wade. Wade, an Englishman, lived in the English colony of Douay, France, where he carried on the business of music copying. At that time it was common for wealthy Catholic families to have their own private chapels and to pay laymen or priests, such as Wade, to compose and copy music for their use. The Duke of Leeds heard *Adeste Fideles* sung at the Portuguese Chapel in London; hence it is frequently referred to as "The Portuguese Hymn."

Certainly it is not difficult to find Wade's well loved *Adeste Fideles* in the hymnals of all Christian denominations and the Latin version is somewhat accessible on popular recordings of Christmas music. The parentage of many other familiar hymns, if the fine print is studied, is Latin, usually of the medieval period. The writing of Latin hymns, however, did not die out with the waning of the medieval period, for both the Renaissance and the Roman Church strongly influenced the continued use of Latin verse forms. Beginning in the sixteenth century, however, the texts of many of the medieval hymns were subject to various reform movements. The Breviary was edited time and again, often to the detriment of the original, as the humanists emended both the prose and poetry to achieve a purer, classical literary style. To cite one example, the humanist pope Urban VIII, in

1629, appointed a commission of four Jesuits to "correct" the hymns, a task which they carried out with zeal, making 952 alterations in eighty-one hymns of the Breviary. Winfred Douglas in *Church Music in History and Practice* provides an original seventh century hymn, then its new "corrected" version:

Angularis fundamentum
    Lapis Christus missus est,
Qui parietum compage
    In utroque nectitur,
Quem Sion sancta suscepit,
    In quo credens permanet.
	Christ is made the sure foundation,
	    Christ the head and corner-stone,
	Who, the two walls underlying
	    Bound in each, binds both to one:
	Holy Sion's help for ever
	    And her confidence alone.

Corrected text:

Alto ex Olympi vertice Summi Parentis Filius Ceu monte desectus lapis Terras in imas decidens, Domus supernoe, et infimoe, Utrumque junxit angulum.	From the high summit of Olympus came the sovereign Father's Son like a stone cut from the mountain descending to the lowest plains, and joined together either corner of the celestial and lower abodes.

Other Renaissance revisions of the Breviary continued the practice, but fortunately, later scholarship was of an opposite mind and sought to restore the Roman liturgy to its traditional roots. Finally, in 1903, Pius X decreed the restoration of plainchant singing and under his leadership a new chant manual was issued.

In the mid-nineteenth century the Oxford Movement in England, whose aim was to restore High Church ideals to the Anglican liturgy, drew on the Sarum Breviary for its translations of Latin hymns. The Oxford Movement revived interest in plainchant as it promoted a return to a ceremonial rite with a fully sung service. There was, as well, renewed interest in the early polyphonic music of the Anglican tradition, and a revival of early English carol singing.

One man, John Mason Neale, made enormous personal contributions to the nineteenth century restoration of medieval hymns. Dr. Neale's relatively short life (1818-1866) was devoted to the renewal of the Anglican Church, in which his singular talents were employed. His translations from the Latin in *Medieval Hymns and Sequences* (1851) introduced English congregations to the glories of medieval sacred music, and Neale did the same for Greek hymns in his later *Hymns of the Eastern Church*. Not only was Neale's classical scholarship of the highest order, but his ear for melody allowed him to phrase his translations in keeping with the rhythm of the original texts. Many of Neale's translations, used in the popular 1861 collection *Hymns Ancient and Modern*, are found in modern hymn books as well.

One other nineteenth century source of Latin hymns and carols is mentioned in Routley's *The English Carol,* as an interesting and fortuitous discovery by G. J. R. Gordon, an English envoy stationed in Stockholm, who saved seventy-three Latin hymns and carols from obscurity. Gordon brought back to England a volume entitled *Piae Cantiones* which had been printed in Finland in 1582. *Piae Cantiones* was conceived as a collection of European folk songs whose words had been adapted to German and Scandinavian Protestant doctrine, but whose tunes had been preserved unchanged. Gordon turned the book over to John Mason Neale, who then set about writing words for the newly discovered tunes and translating others into English. The familiar carol "Good King Wenceslas" was written by Neale, who wished to compose verses to honor St. Stephen. In *Piae Cantiones* Neale found a tune much to his liking, whose words were a Latin carol to spring, *Tempus adest floridum* (Spring has now unwrapped the flowers). There could hardly be a greater transformation than that from the Latin lyrics in praise of the warmth and flowers of spring to Neale's picture of the snow lying "Deep and crisp and even." The *Oxford Book of Carols* is not so charitable and calls "Wenceslas" one of Neale's less happy creations, stating that the carol is included, "... not without the hope that, with the present wealth of carols for Christmas, 'Good King Wenceslas' may gradually pass into disuse, and the tune be restored into spring-time."

This overview of the development of Latin sacred verse, from the anti-Arian hymns of St. Ambrose through the evolutionary process which religious poetry experienced within the context of the Roman Catholic Mass, is only a glance at a subject somewhat outside the usual focus of a classicist. The intent is to emphasize that the ageless character and beauty of this Latin sacred music, whether in hymn, sequence, or carol, has assured its survival not only within but beyond the Roman Catholic tradition.

Secular Verse

The twelfth century, which saw the rise of the liturgical sequence, was also the century of a new force in Latin secular verse. Until this time secular poetry had clung, with some exceptions, to the classical mode of quantitative verse. From Charlemagne's time through the twelfth century, there were various examples of Latin poetry which exhibited an acccentual form, as in later church hymns, rather than the classical scansion by quantity (syllable length). Much of this accentual lyric poetry was found in a manuscript called the *Cambridge Songs*, a collection of secular verse on a variety of themes, from rhythmical parodies of sacred texts to love songs. The refinement of the rather simple language and rhyme patterns of the *Cambridge Songs* belongs to the Goliards, who appeared in the twelfth century.

The origin of the name Goliard is uncertain. It may have an affinity with the Biblical Goliath; it may be coined from the Latin *gula* or gullet, since

Jan Christoffel Jegher (c. 1618-1666), woodcut from *Emblemata sacra.* Courtesy of Abaris Books, Inc.

the Goliards were notorious gluttons; or there may have been a prototype hero named Golias. In medieval times the term was in common use, often found in ecclesiastical writing as a synonym for wandering scholar. Since many of the scholars had taken minor orders in the Church, they are often referred to also as clerks, *clerici*. Although the church was frequently satirized by the Goliards, the poets, as a group, were in position of dependency on the church and even thought of their fraternity as an Order.

The Goliards were itinerants who lived on the fringes of the Church, which regarded them with considerable animosity; many were, in fact, dropouts from the religious life. The Goliard was the social peer of the troubadour who wrote and performed popular poetry in the vernacular. The Goliard could be, as well, a scholar, part of a widespread community of young men who traveled from university to university in search of knowledge, since it was the nature of medieval learning that different sciences had to be studied in different parts of Europe. A twelfth century monk wrote, "The scholars are wont to roam around the world and visit all its cities, till such learning makes them mad; for in Paris they seek liberal arts, in Orleans authors, at Salerno gallipots {druggists}, at Toledo demons, and in no place decent manners."

One anonymous Goliard, known as the Archpoet, wrote secular verse which, in its technical perfection, compares favorably with the finest of the religious. The Archpoet's most famous verse is the *Confessio Goliae*, so greatly imitated for both its rhythm and its rhyme that the Goliardic meter came into being.

The thirteenth century anthology of Goliardic poetry known as the *Carmina Burana* is primarily responsible for our knowledge of the secular lyrics of this period. The poems included in the *Carmina* range from pieces of the highest artistic standard to thoroughly inelegant verses of little merit. The general themes of the anthology are Crusade poems, satires against the excesses of the Church, love songs, spring songs and obscene verses.

At times Goliardic verse degenerated into blasphemy. As John Addington Symonds points out in *Wine, Women and Song,* the Goliards belonged to the same era which produced the religious fervor of the Crusades, but they viewed the Church as an object of scorn. The pomp of liturgical ceremonies is satirized in the "Drunkard's Mass" in which the word *bibamus,* "Let us drink," took the place of *oremus,* "let us pray;" the benediction was "Fraud be with you," *fraus vobis.*

A Students' Drinking Bout, woodcut, from *Directorium statuum,* c. 1489. Courtesy of Constable & Co., Ltd.

The vagabond Goliards seemed to have been as familiar with the tavern as with the lecture hall, and when they wax eloquent in praise of drinking, they are perhaps truest to their own nature. On the other hand, the students reveal their scholarly background by the many classical allusions in their drinking odes. One of the *Carmina,* entitled *In taberna quando sumus* (When we are in the tavern), brought this observation from Helen Waddell, a British scholar of medieval verse, "It seems not possible that poetry should be as gay as this. These poets are young, as Keats and Shelley and Swinburne never were young, with the youth of wavering branches and running water."

The Goliards are the direct antecedents of all modern vernacular poets. With minds and ears trained to the wonderful Latin hymns of the medieval Church, they secularized the verse forms in praise of wine, youth and love. Robert Frost is quoted in Whicher's *The Goliard Poets* where he acknowledges, in verse, the debt of all poets to the Goliards:

> — singing but Dione in the wood
> And ver aspergit terram floribus
> They slowly led old Latin verse to rhyme
> And to forget the ancient length of time,
> And so began the modern world for us.

For various reasons, the secular music of the Middle Ages has not been preserved so well as sacred music. For one, the manuscripts of the ninth through the eleventh centuries which have survived with melodies employ musical notations called neumes, for which there is no certain method of transcription into modern notation. Since centuries passed before musical notation advanced to the use of the staff and the fixed measurement of time values, the neumes of the secular music remain in a sort of musical limbo. In addition, there had been, over the years, no systematic singing of the secular lyrics, unlike sacred verse, which was a necessary part of the liturgy, used at the same time and in the same way, year in and year out. Secular songs, on the other hand, were transmitted from mouth to mouth and singers then, as now, freely changed the melodies. Furthermore, secular music lacked the great choirs associated with cathedrals and monasteries, which undertook to preserve liturgical music for succeeding generations. Within the Catholic tradition, it would have been regarded as sacrilegious to tamper with the melody of a Gregorian chant. And, finally, the copying of manuscripts was an expensive, laborious process. The trained cleric or layman who worked at transcription, either in a monastery or a royal court, did not copy manuscripts unless they were important to his sponsoring institution. Secular music, as a consequence, did not have that requisite importance either to the church or to the court.

The lack of manuscript melodies for Latin secular verse is a lamentable fact of medieval music. It is unfortunate, too, that lyric verse, abundant though it is, has rarely been used by Renaissance or later composers for choral or vocal compositions. The one eminent exception is the German composer Carl Orff. The 1937 production of his *Carmina Burana* was conceived as a total theatrical experience: music, drama and movement were all wedded to the medieval Latin lyrics. Sketches of the Frankfort opening show that Orff's original production was a visual and musical feast, and it has remained a very popular, often recorded, choral *tour de force*. Although Orff tapped only a fraction of the Goliardic verse, he has given the musical world a rare and marvelous glimpse of the richness of Latin secular poetry of the Middle Ages.

Accentual Verse

It is important to examine the difference between the medieval verse represented by some of the songs in this collection and the Latin verse of the classical period which is the usual model in the Latin classroom. The very earliest Latin verse known took no notice of the length or shortness of syllables. This, the so-called Saturnine meter, the only native Italian verse form, was typified in the verse of the common people, in ditties for the stage, and in the marching songs of soldiers. Thus, a dactyl, in the accentual form, consisted of one accented and two unaccented syllables, not of one long and two short syllables. When the principles of Greek versification began to influence Roman writers, classical Latin poetry took on the quantitative form in which the length of the syllables determined the meter. The Saturnine, or accentual verse, was relegated to the tavern and the marketplace.

In the last centuries of classicism, the gulf between literary Latin and popular Latin widened. Douglas gives this summary of the evolution of the language:

> The sovereign catalyst which blended into homogeneity
> the various elements of primitive Christian song was the
> Latin tongue as it developed from the close of the third
> century to that of the sixth. The majestic language of
> Cicero and Caesar, of Horace and Virgil, had carried on,
> in another medium, the tradition of Greek culture. But
> later, classical Latin became more and more an artificial
> vehicle of preciosity within a limited group of literary men,
> and a younger and more flexible Latin became the speech
> of the people. Both in Greek and Latin, the old learned
> conception of quantity was gradually superseded by the
> new convenience of accent. Practical Latin ceased to be
> metrical and became rhythmical.

Douglas goes on to point out that a similar change took place in Latin prose, which can be seen in early translations of the Bible into Latin, reflecting as they did the popular speech of the time. In order to deal with Old Testament rhythms in the Hebrew or Greek scriptures, Latin had to be released from some of its classical strictures. Raby states, "the mystical fervor of the prophets, the melancholy of the penitential Psalms or of the Lamentations, could not be rendered in Latin without giving that severe and logical language a strange flexibility, an emotional and symbolical quality which had been foreign to its nature."

If the accentual verse form was closer to the popular speech of the masses, an assumption for which there is not universal agreement, then it was the more natural verse form for Christian poetry. Early Christian congregations were, after all, not drawn from the cultured few but generally from the uneducated and underprivileged classes.

Another influence on the accentual trend in medieval verse is the dominance of the musical form. When a verse becomes a melody, a long and a short syllable have the same importance because a musical tone can prolong either type of syllable. Because the great poetic creations of the Middle Ages were invented for the service of the Church, the verse forms which developed were molded to the chant tunes. As polyphonic music developed in the twelfth and thirteenth centuries, singers and listeners alike took more and more pleasure in the regular beat of the music. Indeed, polyphony demanded music with a measured beat. The development of the rhythms and rhymes of the Latin sequences belongs to the same era as the development of measured, polyphonic verse.

William Beare in *Latin Verse and European Song* gives an exhaustive study of the matter of accent and rhythm in Latin verse. He stresses the need for a caveat in the discussion of medieval Latin versification. Because the rhymed verse form seems so much closer to our own sense of poetry, and, therefore, perhaps, so much more intelligible than classical verse, it would be easy to conclude that the medieval form is the long delayed true flowering of Latin poetry. Classical Latin verse must be judged by its own standards. If the Romans imitated Greek quantitative verse forms and forsook the old Saturnine verse, they did so because they preferred the new quantitative form. Vergil was not writing in an alien mode, but in one much admired and understood by his contemporaries. Beare notes that ordinary people attempted to write in the classical meters, as witnessed by the numerous examples of popular verse: graffiti, riddles, proverbs, soldiers' songs, and, especially, funeral inscriptions. When medieval verse flourished, Latin had ceased to be anyone's vernacular speech. It was, to be sure, the language of learning and of written records all over Europe, but it was not the language which people spoke on the streets. Classical poetry was an art form of an age when Latin was the vernacular, and it should be viewed as the noble and eloquent art of its time. Medieval verse is the product of a different age; it is not the ultimate in Latin versification, but, rather, a witness to the amazing vitality and adaptability of the Latin language.

Pronunciation

The pronunciation of the classical period of Latin has not come down to the modern age in its entirety, although the conventions of pronunciation, as set forth in standard textbooks, serve as the contemporary norm. Latin, like all languages, has been subjected to the forces of historical change and linguistic evolution. For musicians, the pronunciation used in the performance of choral Latin is that which survived through the influence of the Roman Catholic Church, typified by the usage of the Italian peninsula where Rome's influence was strongest.

A complete and current pronunciation guide can be found in Ron Jeffers' *Translations and Annotations of Choral Repertoire*, which is an excellent manual for choral directors, not only in matters of pronunciation but of interpretation as well. Jeffers' guide can be summarized as follows:

Vowels:

A as in *father*; **E** as in *fed*; **I** and **Y** as in *feet*; **O** as in *fought*; **U** as in *food*.

Dipthongs are usually given the two separate vowel sounds, except for **AE/OE** which is pronounced like the interjection "eh." **U**, when preceded by Q or NG and followed by another vowel is shortened to the sound of the glide [w]: qui = kwee.

Consonants:

B, D, F, K, L, M, N, P, Q, V are pronounced as in English.

C is hard, as in *kick*, exept before E, AE, OE, I, Y, when pronounced "ch" as in *church*.

CC before the above vowels is "tch" as in *fetch*

SC before the same vowels is "sh" as in *shell*.

CH is always like K.

G is hard, as in *God*, except before E, AE, OE, I, when it is soft as in *gem*.

GN has the sound of "ny" as in *canyon*.

H is silent as in *honest*, except in two medieval glosses, mihi, mee-kee, and nihil, nee-keel.

J like "y" in *you* and it is sometimes written as "i".

PH has an "f" sound.

R should be rolled slightly at the beginning of the word and flipped with the tongue in median positions.

S is hard as in *see*, except slightly softened between two vowels.

SCH as the "sk" of *school*.

T is hard as in *tea*.

TI before a vowel and following any letter except S, X, or J, is pronounced "tsee".

TH is always hard like *tea*.

X as the "ks" in *tacks*, but softened slightly between two vowels.

XC as "ksk" before O, A, or U, but as "ksh" before E, AE, OE, I, Y.

Y is same as the vowel I.

Z as the "dz" of *suds*.

The Virgin's Cradle Hymn

Latin Text:

Dormi Jesu, mater ridet
quae tam dulcem somnum videt—
    Dormi Jesu blandule.
Si non dormis mater plorat—
Inter fila cantans orat,
    Blande veni Somnule!

Published Translation:

Sleep, sweet babe! my cares
    beguiling;
Mother sits beside thee smiling;
    Sleep, my darling, tenderly!
If thou sleep not, mother
    mourneth,
Singing as her wheel she turneth:
    Come, soft slumber, balmily!

Notebook Translation:

Sleep, my Jesu!—Mother's smiling,
Sweetest Sleep thy sense beguiling,
    Sleep, my Jesu! balmily—
If thou sleep not, Mother
    mourneth,
Singing while her Wheel she
    turneth,
    Stay, sweet Slumber, hov'ringly.

Published translation by permission of
Oxford University Press, Inc.
Notebook translation by permission of
Pantheon Books, Inc.

Old engraving. Courtesy of
Dick Sutphen Studio.

Vocabulary

rideo, risi, risum, 2. laugh
ploro, 1. cry, wail, lament
filum, fili N., thread
blandus -a -um, fondling, caressing
somnulus, diminutive of *somnus,* sleep

1

THE VIRGIN'S CRADLE HYMN

This carol was the discovery of the English poet Samuel Taylor Coleridge. As a young man Coleridge had acquired an excellent training in classical scholarship and an enthusiasm for languages. Even in his early years when he was sent to school in London after the death of his father, the fourteen-year-old Samuel belied his reputation as a somewhat dull pupil when he was discovered reading Vergil for his own pleasure. In 1798 he was a young married man with two small children, but he determined, nonetheless, to leave his family in England while he embarked on a trip to Germany with his friends the Wordsworths where he planned to study chemistry and anatomy and complete his mastery of the German tongue.

During his eleven month stay at Gottingen and Ratzeburg, Coleridge, in the spring of 1799, took time away from his more serious pursuits for a week-long

Mattheus Schmid (active c. 1653-1680), *The Virgin and the Sleeping Infant Christ,* woodcut. Courtesy of Abaris Books, Inc.

walking tour in the Hartz Mountains. Coleridge kept notebooks of his random impressions of the local scenery, peculiar native customs, and linguistic curiosities. It is in his notebooks that a penciled copy is found of the Latin "Virgin's Cradle Hymn," prefaced by: "At the bottom of a little Print in a Roman Catholic Village in the electorate of Mentz — May 1799." The village is not clearly identified but the succeeding notebook entry describes two villages, Womarshausen and Gieboldhausen, either of which could be the site of his discovery.

In the Coleridge notebook, just below his handwritten copy of the Latin text, the poet has at the same time given an English translation which may be regarded as quite spontaneous since it appears in his travel journal. Coleridge first published the Latin poem in *The Morning Post* of December 26, 1801, identifying himself as "A Correspondent in Germany."

It was not until ten years later that Coleridge published the Latin and English poems together in the *Courier* of August 30, 1811, with the following introduction:

> About thirteen years ago or more, travelling through the middle parts of Germany I saw a little print of the Virgin and Child in the public house of a Catholic village, with the following beautiful Latin lines under it, which I transcribed. They may be easily adapted to the air of the famous Sicilian Hymn, *Adeste Fideles, laeti triumphantes*, by the omission of a few notes.

The *Oxford Book of Carols* provides "The Virgin's Cradle Hymn" with its own melody, the work of Edmond Rubbra.

Edmond Rubbra (1901-1986) was born at Northhampton, England, into a working-class family, and by his evident musical gifts he earned a scholarship to the Royal College of Music. Various teaching, performing, and writing jobs culminated in a lectureship at Oxford University from 1947 to 1968. Two other English universities, Durham and Leicester, paid tribute to Rubbra with honorary degrees in 1949 and 1959, respectively. Rubbra, one of England's leading musical figures in this century, was a prolific composer whose compositions included eleven symphonies, four masses, and, in addition, many choral and chamber works. When Rubbra copyrighted the music to "The Virgin's Cradle Hymn," in 1926, he was just twenty-five years old, and the tune is numbered opus 3 in his collected works.

The obituary tribute to Rubbra in the August, 1986 issue of *High Fidelity* magazine by Robert R. Reilly is a eulogy of the composer and his work, stating, in part:

> ... the ugliness of much of our art is a reflection of the spiritual malaise of our time, not of a horror surpassing, say, that of the Black Death. It may well come as a revelation to archaeologists of the 20th century that many more hardy souls than imagined refused to succumb to this regnant malaise, but continued in obscurity to create works of wholeness. It will take some digging to find out who they were because they were ignored by their tastemaking contemporaries: They were considered "reactionary." We have just lost one of those reactionaries. His name was Edmund Rubbra... and he wrote beautiful music.

SONG OF THE NUNS OF CHESTER

LATIN TEXT:	TRANSLATION:

Qui creavit coelum,
Lully, lully, lu,
Nascitur in stabulo,
By, by, by, by, by,
Rex qui regit seculum,
Lully, lully, lu.

He who created the heaven
Is born in a stable,
The king who rules the world

Joseph emit paniculum,
Lully, lully, lu,
Mater involvit puerum,
By, by, by, by ,by,
Et ponit in praesepio,
Lully, lully, lu.

Joseph buys the swaddling clothes,
The Mother wraps the babe
And places him in the manger.

Inter animalia,
Lully, lully, lu,
Iacent mundi gaudia,
By, by, by, by, by,
Dulcis super omnia,
Lully, lully, lu.

Among the animals
Lies all earthly joy,
The sweetest joy of all.

Lactat mater domini,
Lully, lully, lu.
Osculatur parvulum,
By, by, by, by, by,
Et adorat dominum,
Lully, lully, lu.

The Mother suckles the Lord,
She kisses the babe
And worships her Lord.

Roga mater filium,
Lully, lully, lu.
Ut det nobis gaudium,
By, by, by, by, by
In perenni gloria,
Lully, lully, lu.

O Mother, ask your son
To give us joy,
In everlasting glory.

In sempiterna saecula,
Lully, lully, lu.
In eternum et ultra,
By, by, by, by, by,
Det nobis sua gaudia,
Lully, lully, lu.

Unto ages of ages,
To eternity and beyond,
May he grant us his grace.

5

VOCABULARY

stabulum, stabuli N., stall, stable, animal shelter
seculum, seculi N., generation, age, an indefinitely long time
paniculus, paniculi N. (dim. of *pannus*), small piece of cloth, swaddling cloth
praesepium, praesepii N., enclosure, crib, manger
osculor, i. dep., to kiss

Barthel Beham (1502-1540),
The Country Fair at Mögeldorff, woodcut.
Courtesy of Hacker Art Books, Inc.

Song of the Nuns of Chester

This charming lullaby belongs to the cathedral town of Chester in northwest England. As Latin teachers are wont to point out, there are various place names in England which are derived from the Latin word for camp, *castra*, and Chester is the prime example. During most of the Roman occupation Chester was the headquarters of one of the three occupying legions of Britain. In medieval times it was a prosperous walled city of artisans and tradesmen and the site of a Catholic bishopric, as well as several lesser churches of historic interest. Among the latter was St. Mary-on-the-Hill, founded in the late twelfth century, incorporating a Benedictine nunnery which housed the treasured relic of the girdle of the martyred St. Thomas à Becket.

Medieval Chester was one of four English cities associated with the production of a unique form of religious drama, the mystery plays. The first evidence of a religious play in Chester was that of a processional, perhaps with tableaux integrated into the ceremony, which was held in 1422 for the feast of Corpus Christi. Later in the century the processional gave way to true theatrical plays and the date was shifted to Whitsuntide (Pentecost). Mystery plays were popular religious entertainment which dealt with events in the life of Christ or with Old Testament themes. The full cycle of Chester plays occupied three successive days, nine plays on Monday, nine on Tuesday, and seven on Wednesday, although the total number of plays did not remain constant over the years. The plays were performed in the open on movable stages which were, in fact, heavy carts which could be pulled through the city to various crossroads, the performances having been well advertised by the town crier and by published banns, or announcements, of the special features of the productions.

Rather than being an ecclesiastical event, the Chester Mysteries were a total civic endeavor with which the mayor's name was prominently associated, and whose production expenses were undertaken by the various craft guilds of the city. The Church was, to be sure, not indifferent to the mysteries and generally tolerated, perhaps even welcomed, this external reinforcement of the church's moral and dogmatic message. There was a tradition, no longer regarded as historically accurate, that the Pope had promised a thousand days pardon to those faithful who attended the whole cycle. With the coming of Anglicanism, however, there was no longer even tolerance for the mysteries, but rather an active antagonism which brought about an end to the cycle in 1575.

From the several manuscript texts for the Chester and other mystery plays, there is evidence of the important role which music played in the dramas, as the texts contain directions for vocal and instrumental music. In addition, the account books of the Chester guilds specify payments to minstrels, singers, and musicians, as well as the renting of instruments. The music was an integral part of the performance, contributing to the total dramatic impact of the mysteries upon the listeners. Two other selections included in this recording also have an association with the plays: *Ave Regina coelorum* was used both at York and Coventry and Coventry and *Non Nobis Domine* at Coventry.

Although in several books of English carols the *Song of the Nuns of Chester* is listed as being a part of the Chester mysteries, a thorough search of current scholarship on the medieval religious drama and the use of music therein yields no reference to this particular song. The association, however, becomes more evident when the *Nuns of Chester* is placed within the context of being a carol, for, in addition to the music which was integrated into the mystery plays, carols were sung as interludes between the scenes of the mysteries. William J. Phillips in his work on the connection of carols with mystery plays notes that:

> ...after a time these carol-interludes became so popular
> with the audience that there was often great rivalry
> between the actors and the carol-singers, and the
> audience, having taken a great liking to the carols, were
> always asking (like Oliver Twist) for more, and it is
> recorded that, at Chester, the audience once wrecked the
> stage and properties and beat the players because they did
> not get enough carols to please them!

It seems unlikely that this sentimental lullaby could have occasioned any such boisterous outburst, but the concept of the carol-interlude may provide a connection between the nuns of St. Mary's and the mystery pageants at Chester.

Both the text and the tune of the *Song of the Nuns of Chester* were found in the nunnery's *Processional* which dates to the fifteenth century. A later printing occurred in a collection by the Henry Bradshaw Society, which was founded in 1890 for the purpose of printing liturgical manuscripts and rare editions of books and documents relating to the history of the Church of England. In 1928 the song made its way into the *Oxford Book of Carols* where it appears with this note appended to the Latin text: "This lullaby, in which the nuns of St. Mary's gave vent to their womanly instincts, would only lose by translation." It is curious that the *Oxford* carol contains the suggestion that the verse be sung by "Two boys" and the refrain by a chorus.

The musical genre of the carol has a very strong historical association with dance. Ultimately, this association may go back to the ancient Greek *choros*, a kind of circling dance of the Attic drama, although the Latin *corolla*, a garland or ring, is also suggested as the source of the term. The medieval origin of the carol is linked to St. Francis, who, in 1223, placed a Christmas crib, or crèche, in his parish church at Graecia, Italy, to make a visual reference to the Christmas story. The common folk responded to the crib tableau with greater interest than to the usual liturgical rites of the church's Nativity celebration, and the carol-dance around the crib was the result. Both the carol and the medieval mystery plays were a popular reaction to the formalism of the church, which, as the *Oxford Book of Carols* states "... had for so many centuries suppressed the dance and the drama, denounced communal singing, and warred against the tendency of the people to disport themselves in church on the festivals."

In its musical form a carol typically begins with a refrain called a *burden* which was repeated after each stanza. Many of the old English carols contain Latin phrases, in macaronic form, either in the verses or in the burden, such as *Gloria in excelsis Deo.* The *Nuns of Chester* is a macaronic carol in that the Latin lines are interspersed with the lullaby refrain which is in English. Although the *Oxford* editors thought a translation superfluous, one has been provided all the same. The melody is from the original Chester manuscript. When the *Nuns of Chester* was included in the *Oxford Book of Carols* it featured the addition of harmonies by the English organist and scholar, John Henry Arnold (1887-1956). Arnold devoted much of his scholarship to the Plainsong and Medieval Music Society and the Church Music Society of England, and his accompaniments are found in two English hymnals.

Orientis Partibus

Latin Text:

[Lux hodie, lux laetitiae! Me judice,
    tristis
Quisquis erit removendus erit
    sollemnibus istis.
Sint hodie procul invidiae, procul
    omnia maesta!
Laeta volunt quicumque colunt
    asinaria festa!]

Orientis partibus
Adventavit Asinus,
Pulcher et fortissimus,
Sarcinis aptissimus.
Hez, Sir Asnes, hez!
Hez, hez, hez, Sir Asnes, hez!

Hic in collibus Sychem,
Iam nutritus sub Ruben
Transiit per Iordanem
Saliit in Bethleem.
Hez, hez, Sir Asnes, hez!

Saltu vincit hinnulos,
Dammas et capreolos,
Super dromedarios
Velox Madieneos.
Hez, hez, Sir Asnes, hez!

Aurum de Arabia,
Thus et myrram de Saba
Tulit in Ecclesia
Virtus Asinaria.
Hez, Sir Asnes, hez!
Hez, hez, hez,
Sir Asnes, hez!

Translation:

[For us today the theme is light,
Brightness alone is our delight.
As I'm the judge, the gloomy face
Is banished from this festive place.
Let jealousies be gone today
And every sadness far away!
Whoever joins the donkey fest,
Has cast his lot for merriment.]

Out from lands of Orient
Was the ass divinely sent.
Strong and very fair was he,
Bearing burdens gallantly.
Heigh, sir ass, oh heigh.

In the hills of Sichem bred
Under Reuben nourishèd.
Jordan stream he traversèd,
Into Bethleem he sped.
Heigh, heigh!

Higher leaped than goats can
    bound,
Doe and roebuck circled round,
Median dromedaries' speed
Overcame, and took the lead.
Heigh, heigh!

Red gold from Arabia,
Frankincense and, from Sheba,
Myrrh he brought and, through the
    door,
Into the Church he bravely bore.
  Heigh, heigh!

11

Dum trahit vehicula,
Multa cum sarcinula,
Illius mandibula
Dura terit pabula.
Hez, hez, Sir Asnes, hez!

While he drags long carriages
Loaded down with baggages,
He, with jaws insatiate,
Fodder hard doth masticate.
Heigh, heigh!

Cum aristis ordeum
Comedit et carduum;
Triticum a palea
Segregat in area.
Hez, hez, Sir Asnes, hez!

Chews the ears with barley corn,
Thistle down with thistle corn,
On the threshing floor his feet
Separate the chaff from wheat.
Heigh, heigh!

Amen dicas, Asine,
Iam satur ex gramine;
Amen, Amen, itera,
Aspernare vetera.
Hez, hez Sir Asnes, hez!

Stuffed with grass, yet speak
    and say
Amen, ass, with every bray:
Amen, amen, say again:
Ancient sins hold in disdain.

Translation is from Greene's article in
Speculum.

———————————•◦•———————————

VOCABULARY

solemne, solemnis N., solemn feast, rite
invidia, invidiae F., envy, jealousy
sarcina, sarcinae F., bundle, pack, burden
nutrio, nutrire, or *nutrior* (dep.), to nourish, bring up
hinnulus, diminutive of *hinnus, hinni* M., a young roebuck, deer
damma, dammae F., fallow-deer, antelope
capreolus, capreoli M., roebuck
thus, tus, turis N., incense, frankincense
mandibula, mandibulae F., jaw
tero, terere, trivi, tritum, to rub, wear away
pabulum, pabuli N., food, fodder
arista, aristae F., beard of an ear of grain
ordeum/ hordeum, hordei N., barley
comedo, comesse, comedi, comestum, consume, eat up

carduus, cardui M., thistle
triticum, tritici N., wheat
pallea/ palea, paleae F., chaff
area, areae F., courtyard, threshing floor
satur -a -um, full, sated
gramen, graminis N., grass, plant, herb
aspernor, 1. to despise, spurn, reject
vetera, veterum N.pl., the remote past, antiquity

The Flight into Egypt,
woodcut, from Geistliche
Auslegung des Lebens
Jesu Christi, c. 1480.
Courtesy of Constable
& Co., Ltd.

ORIENTIS PARTIBUS

This hymn's performance was associated with the custom of some medieval towns to celebrate, through a religious pageant, the episode of the Holy Family's flight into Egypt. Rather than the Holy Family, strangely, it was the donkey which became the central figure in the celebration, giving rise to a special song in praise of the honored beast, *Orientis Partibus*.

The so-called "Prose of the Ass" must be viewed in a larger context, however, that of a less than solemn religious holiday referred to as the Feast of Fools. In some medieval cathedrals, almost exclusively in France, the fortnight following Christmas was the occasion of special festivities under the direction of different ranks of the clergy, called variously *festum stultorum*, *fatuorum* or *follorum*. E. K. Chambers, who devotes two chapters to the Feast of Fools in his work *The Medieval Stage*, finds the Feast mentioned for the first time in church documents from the end of the twelfth century. The two main sites for which manuscripts exist containing the "Prose of the Ass" are the French cities of Beauvais and Sens.

A thirteenth century manuscript from Sens offers a choirbook entitled *Missel des Fous* (Book of Fools), for use in the chants of the Hours and the Mass on the Feast of Circumcision, January 1. In the manuscript the first Vespers on the eve of the Feast has a four-line preface, with instructions that it was sung *in ianuis ecclesiae* (at the church doors). These are the opening lines of the hymn *Orientis Partibus* and they are an invitation to lay aside gloom, jealousies and sadness and join in the gaiety of the donkey festival.

14

In the cathedral town of Beauvais, early in the thirteenth century, a similar drama was performed. A manuscript in the British Museum, dating to the pontificate of Gregory IX (1217-1240), contains the text of the "Prose of the Ass." An account of the Beauvais celebration was found in a letter, dated December 18, 1697, which has been reproduced by Henry Copley Greene in an article on "The Song of the Ass" in *Speculum*, a journal of Medieval Studies.

> On the first day of the Octave of the [three] Kings, they chose a beautiful young girl, put a child in her hands, and mounted her on an ass which they led in procession from the Cathedral Church to the Church of St. Stephen. Placing the ass and his lovely burden in the Sanctuary there on the Gospel side, they sang a solemn mass, whose prose [of the Ass] is in Louvet, and whose *Introit*, *Kyrie*, *Gloria*, *Credo*, etc., end in *hin ham* [he haw], to the point where *in fine missae sacerdos versus ad populum vice "Ite, Missa est ter hinhanabit* [he-hawed], *populus vero vice 'Deo gratias' ter respondavit, "'Hin-ham, Hinham, Hinham'"*.

In the letter quoted above, the Louvet referred to is Pierre Louvet who wrote a seventeenth century history of Beauvais. The Latin quotation is translated: "at the end of the mass the priest, turning to the people, having said 'Go, it is the dismissal,' he-hawed three times; then the people, having said, 'Thanks be to God,' responded three times, 'He-haw'". An earlier manuscript from Beauvais recorded the censing of the cathedral with the burning of blood-pudding and sausage, "Hic die incensabitur cum boudino et saucisa."

During the twelfth through the fifteenth centuries, church documents speak out against the Feast of Fools which had become a scandal to the ecclesiastical authorities. About 1400, the rector of Paris University campaigned against *ritus ille impiissimus et insanus qui regnat per totam Franciam* (that most sacrilegious and insane ritual which pervades all of France).

Chambers discusses the scant evidence linking the Feast of Fools to the pagan Kalends of January which had come into Gaul with the spread of the Roman Empire. He writes of the Kalends:

> Up to the eighth century a fast, with its mass *pro prohibendo ab idolis*, it gradually took on a festal character, and became ultimately the one feast in the year in which paganism made its most startling and persistent recoil upon Christianity.

Chambers offers, in addition, interesting information on the persistent image of the donkey in Christian symbolism.

Two different early melodies were known from the manuscripts, both of which have been transcribed and revised, with changes both in time and key introduced by later musicians. The melody *Orientis Partibus* made its way into the 1909 edition of *Hymns Ancient and Modern* and into many other hymnals where the tune is frequently used with the hymn "Soldiers Who are Christ's Below." The performance text published by Oxford University Press in *Now Make We Merthe* incorporates verses from several manuscript sources, although it does not include the four line preface of the Sens choirbook.

MIRABILE MYSTERIUM AND
O ADMIRABLE COMMERCIUM

Mirabile mysterium declaratur hodie,
innovantur naturae:
Deus homo factus est.
Id, quod fuit, permansit,
et quod non erat, assumpsit:
non commixtionem passus,
neque divisionem.

A wonderful mystery is revealed
   today:
The two natures are renewed:
God has become man.
That which He was, He remained,
and that which He was not,
   He assumed:
suffering neither mixture
nor division.

The translation is from Jeffers'
*Translations and Annotations of Choral
Repertoire*, Vol. I: *Sacred Latin Texts*.

LATIN TEXT:

TRANSLATION:

O admirabile commercium!
Creator generis humani,
animatum corpus sumens,
de Virgine nasci dignatus est:
et procedens homo sine semine,
largitus est nobis suam deitatem.

O wondrous interchange!
The Creator of the human race,
assuming a living body,
has deigned to be born of a virgin;
and issuing forth unbegotten,
He has bestowed upon us His divinity.

VOCABULARY

commixtio, commixtionis F., a mixing together
commercium, commercii N., trade, commerce, communication
largior, largiri, largus/largitus, to give abundantly

O Admirable Commercium and Mirabile Mysterium

Both of these Christmas songs are from the pen of the Renaissance composer, Jacob Handl. Their theme is the great and wondrous mystery of the Savior's birth. The texts are drawn from the Roman Catholic liturgical chants associated with the Feast of the Circumcision. This ancient religious day of celebration was traditionally observed eight days after Christmas, on January 1, following the Biblical account of Christ's presentation in the temple on the eighth day after his nativity. In the sixth century the feast appeared among the Christians of Spain and Gaul; it spread slowly until, in the eleventh century, it was firmly established in Rome. A possible explanation for its relatively late acceptance by the Church was Rome's reluctance to countenance any celebration on January 1. The New Year's Day had very strong pagan overtones as a festival of riotous merry-making and early Christian writers attacked the Kalends of January revelries, which had become even more boisterous than the Saturnalia. (See *Orientis Partibus*.) The

Albrecht Dürer (1471-1528), *The Adoration of the Magi*, woodcut. Courtesy of Dover Publications, Inc.

18

earliest liturgy for January 1 was an ancient mass, *Missa ad prohibendum ab idolis* (a mass for protection from idols), a stern statement against the pagan holiday. In Handl's day the Feast of the Circumcision still held its place in the church calendar, but over the centuries it too gave way; as of 1961, January 1 has been officially designated as the Octave of Christmas, a Marian feast, by the Roman Catholic Church.

Jacob Handl or **Jacobus Gallus** (1550-1591) was born in Slovenia, formerly part of Yugoslavia. He may have had a third name as well, Petelin, the native word for rooster, for which the German equivalent is Handl and the Latin, Gallus. Handl received a monastic education in Slovenia and later at Vienna, where for a time he was a singer at the court of Emperor Maximillian II. The remainder of his life was spent in a succession of ecclesiastical posts as choirmaster, soloist, or teacher. Handl was a contemporary of Palestrina and Lassus, both great figures of late Renaissance music.

Handl's musical output was prodigious: he composed twenty masses and 445 motets, a complete cycle of music for the church year. For the most part Handl's religious works are settings of sacred Latin texts, either from the Bible or from the manuals of the Roman liturgy. Handl's genius for harmony led him beyond the usual settings for four vocal parts, as he scored many of his motets for eight voices, or double choirs; and, in some cases, he supported the singers with organ or other instrumental accompaniment. Through shifts of pitch and pattern, Handl used the human voice to achieve an almost orchestral range. *Mirabile mysterium* is an example of his harmonic writing that is, as Allen Skei describes it, "unrivaled in its chromatic complexity by any of Handl's other compositions."

A poetic tribute to Handl's virtuosity in vocal harmonics, written two years after Handl's death by Henricus Goetting, is printed in translation from the original German in Skei's article on Handl's polychordal music in *Music Review*:

Jacobus Handl Carniolus
Was a musician also called Gallus.
Much had he written in a few years
For just as in a verdant wood
The birds among themselves do sing
So that their song towards us might wing,
Our Handl many motets has penned
Toward man much joy and love to send.
Is there a man whose soul and heart
His music can't touch, if only in part?
Wholly of stone that man must be
Whose heart can't Handl's greatness see.
So, then, our God we thank and praise,
Who gladdens our hearts in troubled days,
With chords arranged so beauteously
To sing and play right variously.

In *The Liturgy of the Hours According to the Roman Rite, O admirabile commercium* is an antiphon for Vespers of the Octave of Christmas, and *Mirabile mysterium* is to be sung at the benediction at the Matins service.

Old engraving from
Dick Sutphen Studio.

Ave Regina Coelorum

Latin Text:

Ave regina caelorum
Ave domina angelorum;
Salve radix, salve porta,
Ex qua mundo lux est orta.

Gaude virgo gloriosa,
Super omnes speciosa;
Vale, o valde decora
Et pro nobis Christum exora.

Dufay's Text:

Ave regina coelorum,
Ave Domina Angelorum:
Salve radix sancta,
Ex qua mundo lux est orta:

Gaude gloriosa,
Super omnes speciosa:
Vale, valde decora,
Et pro nobis semper
Christum exora. Alleluia.

Translation:

Hail, queen of heaven;
Hail, mistress of the angels;
Hail, root of Jesse; hail, the gate
Through which the Light rose
Over the earth.

Rejoice, virgin most renowned
And of unsurpassed beauty.
Farewell, lady most comely.
Prevail upon Christ to pity us.

The translation is from Connelly's
Hymns of the Roman Liturgy.

Albrecht Dürer, *The Virgin Mary
in the Sun,* woodcut. Courtesy of
Hacker Art Books, Inc.

Vocabulary:

caelum/coelum, coeli, N., heaven
radix, radicis, F., root
mundus, mundi, M., world
orior, oriri, ortum, rise, to appear
speciosus -a -um, beautiful, splendid
valde, strongly, intensely, very
decorus -a -um, becoming, proper,
   decorous

21

AVE REGINA COELOROM

Ave *Regina Coelorum* is one of four medieval compositions known collectively as the Marian Antiphons *(antiphonae B.M.V., that is Beatae Mariae Virginis).* The term Marian refers, of course, to the Virgin Mary. The term antiphon, on the other hand, from which our word anthem is derived, has neither a short nor a simple definition. It was originally a brief chant to be sung at the beginning or the end of the reading of a psalm, or as a refrain after each psalm verse. Although some antiphons were associated with the Mass, the greater number were used during the Offices of the monastic day. In number the Office Antiphons are counted in the thousands in various medieval sources. As the evolutionary process of liturgical music is exceedingly complex, each individual type mirrors this development from simplicity to increasing complexity. By the thirteenth century the simple antiphon as a psalm chant had become highly ornate and polyphonic, nor was it any longer associated solely with the reading of the psalm.

The eminent musicologist Willi Apel writes that the four Antiphons in praise of the Blessed Virgin are among the most beautiful creations of the late Middle Ages. Many chants on this theme were in use from the eleventh century on, but only the four Marian Antiphons have a place in modern church usage: *Ave Regina coelorum, Alma Redemptoris Mater, Regina caeli laetare,* and *Salve Regina.* Each of the four antiphons is assigned to one of the four seasons of the church year, *Ave Regina* being employed from February 2, the feast of the Purification of the Blessed Virgin, also known as Candlemas Day, until the Wednesday of Holy Week.

Only one of the Marian Antiphons, *Alma Redemptoris,* has an established authorship, that of Hermannus Contractus (1013-54). An exact date of composition of *Ave Regina,* on the other hand, is unknown, but dating can be noted in terms of manuscript evidence. In the British Museum collection *Ave Regina* is found in the twelfth century *St. Alban's Book* and in a *Sarum Breviary* of the fourteenth century. In 1249, the Marian Antiphons are mentioned collectively in a letter written by the Franciscan minister general, John of Parma, to the friars Minor, instructing them in the use of the Breviary of Aymo.

The companion Marian Antiphon *Alma Redemptoris* was evidently well-known in England in the Middle Ages, for Chaucer used it as the theme of "The Prioress's Tale". It tells of a young Christian boy who had memorized both the words and music of the antiphon and it had become his custom to sing it on his journey to and from school:

> *Ful murily than wolde he synge and crie*
> *O* Alma redemptoris *evermo.*

The youth's journey along the public streets took him through the Jewish section of the town where he was apprehended, his throat cut, and his body thrown into a pit. When his mother found her missing son, the mutilated body continued to sing:

> *There he with throte ykorvan lay upright,*
> *He* Alma redemptoris *gan to synge*
> *So loude that al the place gan to rynge.*

So he continued to sing his anthem until his captors cut out his tongue and death at last brought silence. Chaucer reflected the unfortunate anti-Jewish sentiment which is found in much of medieval literature.

The Reverend John Connelly has noted that the original verse of the *Ave Regina* was not in metrical form, but was later adapted for its seasonal use into its present trochaic trimeter, with the two opening dactylic lines. The poetic structure consists of two pairs of similar phrases followed by an unmatched pair. The word *radix* refers to Mary as a root, that is the root of the houses of Jesse and David, from which Christ was descended. The word *porta,* gate, has two possible interpretations: the Virgin as the gate of heaven, a common metaphor, or as the gate of the morning, which thematically is closer to *"lux est orta."*

Guillermus (Guillaume) Dufay was born in Hainault, France, about 1400. He received his musical education at Cambrai, an important cathedral city near the border of France and Belgium, whose music school had an outstanding reputation in Europe. Dufay was a prolific composer of sacred and secular works, produced during a succession of posts in Belgium, France, and Italy. His biographer, David Fallows, opens his study, "Dufay now stands unchallenged as the leading composer of the Middle Ages." In his own time, furthermore, Dufay was similarly revered, in the era of such artists as Botticelli, Brunelleschi, Donatello, and the brothers Van Eyck. Fallows notes that, in 1467, his contemporary Piero de' Medici praised Dufay as "the greatest ornament of our age."

Although Dufay composed a large number of secular songs both in French and Italian, his regular employment as a church musician gives the preponderance to his sacred works. There are three separate compositions from Dufay's pen for the antiphon *Ave Regina;* the earliest is the three-part motet of this recording, composed about 1426. The three-voice polyphony of the motet has simple chordal structure, lacking the more elaborate harmonies which the addition of the bass voice would intensify. Late in Dufay's life he composed another *Ave Regina* motet in four parts, and his last mass, also an *Ave Regina.* Evidently Dufay felt a great personal identification with the four-part motet because he requested in his will that it be chanted over his death-bed. For this solemn occasion a supplication for his own mercy was inserted into the text, *"Miserere tui labentis Dufay"* (have mercy on your sinner Dufay). The will stated that the antiphon was to be sung by choir boys with three men, if time permitted, but the account left by his executor stated that death came too rapidly to fulfill his wish and the antiphon was sung along with the Requiem Mass at Dufay's funeral.

The usual text is given, as found in standard church collections, along with the translation of The Reverend Joseph Connelly, from his book *Hymns of the Roman Liturgy*. The text of Dufay's motet varies slightly from the hymnal version.

Hans Holbein the Elder c. 1465-1524), *The Virgin with Her Protective Raiment,* woodcut. Courtesy of Hacker Art Books, Inc.

Ave Generosa

     Translation:

Ave, generosa,
gloriosa
et intacta puella;
tu, pupilla castitatis,
tu, materia sanctitatis,
que Deo placuit!

Hail, Thou noble maiden,
Thou glorious and unblemished one.
Thou, the pupil of purity's eye,
Thou, the wellspring of holiness,
Who hast found favor with God!

Nam hec superna infusio
in te fuit,
quod supernum verbum
in te carnem induit,

In Thee God's grace was
    consummate,
In Thee God's word was incarnate.

Tu, candidum lilium,
quod Deus ante omnem creaturam
inspexit.

How has the Lord regarded Thee,
Oh radiant lily,
Before every living thing!

O pulcherrima et dulcissima;
quam valde Deus in te delectabatur!
cum amplexione caloris sui
in te posuit ita quod filius eius
de te lactatus est.

O most beautiful
And most cherished maiden,
How greatly has the Lord delighted
    in Thee!
With the embrace of His own fervor
He has implanted in Thee,
So that His Son might nurse
    at Thy breast.

Venter enim tuus
gaudium habuit,
cum omnis celestis symphonia
de te sonuit,
quia, virgo, filium Dei portasti,
ubi castitas tua in Deo claruit.

For when Thy womb held our joy,
Every heavenly voice joined
In a symphony of praise;
For when Thou, oh maid, did bear
    God's son,
In His sight Thy chastity did blaze.

Viscera tua gaudium habuerunt,
sicut gramen super quod ros cadit
cum ei viriditatem infudit;

Thy flesh received the joy
As the grass receives the dew,
With showers that make it new;

ut et in te factum est,
o mater omnis gaudii.

So, oh Mother of every joy,
In Thee God's blessing grew.

Nunc omnis Ecclesia
in gaudio rutilet
ac in symphonia sonet
propter dulcissimam virginem
et laudabilem Mariam
Dei genitricem. Amen.

Now let all the Church
With joy be bright,
And harmony on all alight,
For the sake of the Virgin so dear,
For Mary be praises clear,
For she is ever the birthgiver
of God. Amen.

VOCABULARY

generosus -a -um, of noble birth, excellent
intactus -a -um, untouched, virgin
pupilla, pupillae, diminutive of pupa, F., pupil of the eye
castitas, castitatis F., chastity
supernus, -a -um, celestial
infusio, infusionis F.,
  a pouring in, infusion
amplexio, amplexionis
  F., embrace
calor, caloris M.,
  warmth, heat
lacto, 1. to give milk
clareo, clarere, clarui,
  clarus 2. to shine
viscus, visceris N., inside
  of the body, entrails
ros, roris M., dew
viriditas, viriditatis F.,
  greenness, freshness

Lucas Cranach, the Elder (1472-1553), *Seven Joys of the Virgin,* woodcut. Courtesy of Hacker Art Books, Inc.

AVE GENEROSA

A*ve Generosa* is a hymn to the Virgin Mary which was written by a
twelfth century German mystic, Hildegard of Bingen. Among all the selections on the recording, only here is the author of the text also the identified
composer of the melody. Because Hildegard's music has only recently
become available in a published score, it is rarely heard in recording. Furthermore, since both words and music are by the same person, a woman, *Ave
Generosa* constitutes a unique example of the medieval Latin hymn.

An examination of the life of Hildegard owes much to the scholarship
of the medievalist Peter Dronke who devotes chapters to her work both in
his *Poetic Individuality in the Middle Ages* and in his later volume
Women Writers of the Middle Ages. Hildegard was born in 1098 at
Böckelheim on the River Nahe, the tenth child of a noble family. Almost
all of her life was spent within the confines of Benedictine convents,
mainly at Bingen, near Rupertsburg, in the Rhine Valley, where she served
as abbess until her death at the age of eighty-two in 1179. She wrote
poetry, music, drama, treatises on science and medicine, and the lives of
the saints; and she engaged in diplomatic activities. Underlying all of these
accomplishments, however, was Hildegard the visionary, the mystic, the
prophetess, whose creative gifts were intimately linked with her trance-like
periods of otherworldliness.

In childhood Hildegard had begun to experience visions, which
continued with increased intensity into her adult life. At the urging of her
contemporaries she began to record her visions, setting forth, over the
years, in three books entitled *Scivias*, her mystical visitations and her own
prophetic interpretations. Several *Scivias* manuscripts contain illuminated
miniatures of the visions, which can be dated with sufficient accuracy to

presuppose that the abbess herself oversaw the artist's work. In a modern investigation, Charles Singer has analyzed the vision illuminations in a search for the pathology of their cause, concluding that migraines and hystero-epilepsy were the likely agents. Singer notes that in Hildegard's time ecstatic visions were a common literary device which continued into succeeding centuries.

Hildegard's prophecies were uncommon enough, however, to bring her considerable repute in Europe. The "Sibyl of the Rhine" was consulted by popes, emperors, kings, archbishops, and lesser clergy with whom she carried on extensive correspondence. Such was her intimacy with the Emperor Frederick Barbarossa that she sent him a chiding letter when, in 1164, he had set up his own anti-pope. She castigated the emperor, as Dronke notes, for behaving "childishly, like one whose model of life is insane *(velut parvulum et velut insane viventem)*."

Hildegard's contemporary biographer, the monk Theodoric, describes the abbess' treatment of the sick for which she is sometimes credited with being a pioneer of the hospital system. She wrote a book on medical practice, *Causae et Curae*, as well as a treatise on natural history, *Physica*. One further innovation is attributed to Hildegard: a morality play, *Ordo Virtutum*, which is the earliest, by more than a hundred years, of this form of religious drama. The *Ordo* describes the struggle between the Virtues and the devil, and it contains eighty-two separate melodies to accompany the text. Finally, Hildegard allowed herself the diversion of creating an unknown language, of which nine hundred words and a made-up alphabet survive. The words seem to be an amalgam of Latin and German, with the addition of the letter "z" to the word endings.

Hildegard's poetry is infused with her visionary imagery and the mystic herself referred to her poetic texts as *Symphonia armonie celestium revelationum* (a symphony of the harmony of heavenly revelations). One form of her poetic compositions, the sequences, surpasses the rest in spontaneity; unlike the sequences of her contemporaries which conformed to a regular strophic pattern, Hildegard's sequences display spontaneous changes in metric pattern. The *Symphonia* contained, as well, Hildegard's original musical compositions.

The musical corpus of Hildegard embraces over one hundred songs, all with Latin texts. The largest part of these comprises a liturgical cycle, providing songs for saints' days and feast days of the church year, with local German saints included. The distinguishing feature of Hildegard's music is the freedom of her melodic patterns: her music does not conform to the plainchant tradition and has no direct musical counterpart. In *Style and Symbol* David Hughes conjectures that Hildegard's departure from the musical conventions of the twelfth century may have been due, in part, to the isolated environment of the abbey at Bingen. All the same, Hildegard's originality must be attributed primarily to her extraordinary creative genius.

There is a fascinating anecdote from the final years of Hildegard's life about the event which occasioned the abbess to write a moving treatise on man's spiritual need for music. In the year before her death Hildegard had incurred the disfavor of church officials in Mainz when she allowed a nobleman who had once been excommunicated to be buried within the convent grounds. The clergy ordered her to disinter the body or face excommunication herself. Hildegard held firm in her belief that God's higher authority prohibited the disturbance of a body buried in holy ground. As part of the church's interdict levied against Hildegard, music was expressly forbidden within the convent. Her letter to the authorities is a passionate defense of the soul's longing for melody. Dronke has summarized her message. "The human soul is symphonic, and any symphony of voices and instruments in earth, which is directed heavenwards, is a means of reintegration, of bringing the lost human-heavenly condition alive again." Although the church did not respond immediately to Hildegard's letter, six months before her death the interdict was lifted.

Although numerous attempts were made by medieval popes to have Hildegard canonized, sainthood was not accorded her, although miraculous cures had been attributed to her efforts. In the fifteenth century her name was accepted into the martyrology, the official Roman Catholic catalogue of martyrs and saints, and September 17 is assigned to commemorate her name. In numerous contexts she is referred to as St. Hildegard which reflects the confusion regarding her canonical status.

In her writings Hildegard often referred to herself as *paupercula feminea forma* (poor little womanly figure) and she belittled her own learning and command of the Latin language. This tone of self-deprecation contrasts dramatically with Dronke's assessment of her gifts in *Women Writers of the Middle Ages*:

> ...she writes a Latin that is as forceful and colorful, and at times as subtle and brilliant, as any in the twelfth century; and her learning is often so astounding that (as she gives no source-references) it still sets countless problems to determine all she had read. Her use of language reflects intimately both her febrile vitality and her exultant sense of the beauty of the physical world, the beauty of music, the beauty that is possible in men and women. Bounded in the nutshell at Rupertsburg, she counts herself a queen of infinite space—though she too has bad dreams. The torments, conflicts, nightmares are evoked as intensely as the rays of the living light.

Ave Generosa is part of a recently published score of nine of the sequences and hymns of Hildegard by Christopher Page. The hymn to the Virgin Mary, as Page notes, shows Hildegard's passionate devotion to the Virgin. In the original manuscripts Hildegard's hymns were written in prose form; consequently the arrangement in stanzas, which is found in Page's score, is an attempt to give the hymn the look of poetry. The stanzas, to be sure, do display poetic elements: metaphor, rhyme and poetic language which convey the sensuous tone of the hymn. Because of the original prose form, however, *Ave Generosa* represents a kind of free verse rather than one of the conventional poetic genres.

HODIE CHRISTUS NATUS EST

LATIN TEXT:

Hodie Christus natus est;
hodie Salvator apparuit;
hodie in terra canunt Angeli,
    laetantur Archangeli;
hodie exsultant iusti
    dicentes:
Gloria in excelsis Deo.
Alleluia, alleluia.

TRANSLATION:

Christ is born today;
today the Saviour has revealed
    himself;
today the angels sing on earth,
    the archangels rejoice;
today the just exult,
    saying:
Glory be to God on high,
Alleluja, alleluja.

Heinrich Aldegrever
(1502-1561), *The Virgin
in a Circular Frame,* woodcut.
Courtesy of Hacker Art Books, Inc.

HODIE CHRISTUS NATUS EST

The text is found in the *Liber Usualis* as an antiphon for the *Magnificat* at Vespers on the day of The Nativity of Our Lord. In describing a text as coming from one of the service books of the Roman Catholic Church, the terminology may presume a knowledge of Catholic practice which few possess, even though many terms can be interpreted in a general way through Latin cognates.

There are many sources for reading in depth about the liturgy of the Catholic Church and its relationship to the development of music. For an excellent overview of the subject, Richard Hoppin's *Medieval Music* serves admirably. Hoppin opens the chapter on "Christian Liturgy:"

> The history of Western music, at least for the first thousand years of the Christian era, must of necessity be a history of the Christian liturgy. Although secular music of various sorts must have existed during this long period of time, almost none has been preserved. Only the chants of the Church remain.

To return to the opening sentence regarding the text of *Hodie Christus natus est*, The *Liber Usualis* (Common Book) is the single volume which contains the prefaces, readings, chants, and hymns of the Latin Mass and the Offices. Although it appears to be a compact volume, the 1952 edition runs to almost 2000 pages, and being a pre-Vatican II edition, it is almost entirely in Latin.

The term Mass, refers, of course, to a celebration of communion, and the word comes from the last three words of the dismissal, *Ite, missa est* (Go, it is the dismissal). The term Offices, also known as the Canonical

Hours, refers to a worship service devoted to the singing of psalms, the reading of scripture, and prayer. Until the great changes brought about by Vatican II in the sixties, when the vernacular languages supplanted Latin, the *Liber Usualis* was the universal compendium of service language and music. It contained musical notation for all the chants which had been prepared under the supervision of the Benedictine monks of Solesmes monastery in France.

The Roman Mass, writes Hoppin, "has occasioned the composition of more music by more composers than any other liturgical service." The sixteenth century Italian composer Palestrina, for example, composed 104 Masses, and the tradition continued through the period of grand symphonic Masses for orchestra and chorus, down to the contemporary Mass of Leonard Bernstein (1970-71). The Offices, too, are also a rich source of music, since they are eight in number and are associated with all the solemn and festal days of the church year. The first listing of the complete cycle of daily offices appears in the Rule of St. Benedict, dating from about 530 A.D.. The Offices are:

1. Matins   Sometime after midnight
2. Lauds   At daybreak
3. Prime (first hour) 6 A.M.
4. Terce (third hour) 9 A.M.
5. Sext (sixth hour)   Noon
6. None (ninth hour)   3 P.M.
7. Vespers   Early evening
8. Compline   Before retiring

When the Office of Vespers was chanted in the early evening, the musical high point was the *Magnificat,* which begins "Magnificat anima mea Dominum" (My soul doth magnify the Lord). The antiphon *Hodie Christus natus est* could be sung both preceding and following the *Magnificat* in the Vesper service.

Just as *Hodie* is specifically assigned to the Office of Vespers, it is also assigned to a particular festive day, the Nativity of Our Lord. A feast day is determined by the calendar, not the usual chronological calendar, but the infinitely more complex church calendar. The church year, or liturgical year, consists of two separate cycles which run concurrently. The first is called the Proper of the Time and allows for all the Sundays of the year, as well as for the important events in Christ's life, namely the Nativity and the Resurrection. Although the Nativity is a fixed date, the Easter festival is a shifting date.

Heironymus Bosch (1450?-1516),
The Adoration of the Magi, woodcut.
Courtesy of Constable & Co., Ltd.

Since Easter determines the dates of most of the Proper of the Time, this first of the two cycles must be adjusted every year. The second cycle, the Proper of the Saints, is a fixed calendar of the feast days of the saints of the church, including those of the Virgin Mary. The feast days, although fixed, fall on different days of the week each year, so it too, in a sense, is a variable calendar. The liturgical year has two main divisions: the Christmas Cycle and the Easter Cycle, each of which, in turn, has three parts, Preparation, Celebration and Prolongation. Those who have struggled with the complexities of the ancient Roman calendar, which counted backward, not forward, can appreciate the intricacies of the Roman Catholic liturgical calendar.

Hodie Christus natus est has been set to music by the French Catholic composer **Francis Poulenc** (1899-1963). Further biographical information can be found with *Ave verum*. Although Poulenc was a twentieth century composer, his life spanned the pre-Vatican II era, which implies that he knew the Catholic liturgy in its Latin form. When, in 1952, he composed his "Four Christmas Motets", he chose four texts from the Nativity services from the *Liber Usualis*. The other three are entitled *O magnum mysterium*, *Quem vidistis pastores dicite*, and *Videntes stellam*. In the 1952 *Liber,* the Nativity services comprise fifty pages. Perhaps Poulenc heard the antiphon *Hodie Christus natus est* chanted in a French cathedral to the notation of the monks of Solesmes. In his composition of the Christmas Motets, Poulenc has elaborated the beautiful words of the Latin text into a new and joyous musical celebration of the birth of Christ.

Wilhelm Traut (c. 1636-1662), *The Infant Christ as Salvator Mundi,* woodcut. Courtesy of Abaris Books, Inc.

Ubi Caritas

Ubi caritas et amor, Deus ibi est.
Congregavit nos in unum Christi
    amor.
Exsultemus et in ipso iucundemur,
Timeamus et amemus Deum vivum
Et ex corde diligamus nos sincero.

Ubi caritas et amor, Deus ibi est.
Simul ergo cum in unum
    congregamur,
Ne nos mente dividamur caveamus.
Cessent iurgia maligna, cessent lites
Et in medio nostri sit Christus Deus.

Ubi caritas et amor, Deus ibi est.
Simul quoque cum beatis videamus
Glorianter vultum tuum,
    Christe Deus;
Gaudium quod est immensum
    atque probum,
Saecula per infinita saeculorum.

Where love and loving-kindness are together, God is in their midst. Christ's love has gathered us together in one company. Let us then rejoice and take delight in Him; let us fear and love the living God; let us without any reserve or deception love one another.

Where love and loving-kindness are together, God is in their midst. And so let us see that whenever we are gathered together in company, we are not divided from each other in our feelings. Let spite, quarrelling and strife give place and may Christ, who is God, be in our midst.

Where love and loving-kindness are together, God is in their midst. May it be ours in company with the blessed, Christ our God, to see Your face in glory — happiness of immeasurable excellence, through unending ages of ages.

The text and translation are from Connelly's *Hymns of the Roman Liturgy.*

VOCABULARY

caritas, caritatis, F., love, affection
congrego, 1. collect, gather together
exsulto, 1. rejoice exceedingly
iucundo, 1. (post-classical, deponent) rejoice, delight
diligo, diligere, dilexi, dilectum, 3. prize, love, esteem
sincerus, -a, -um, pure, sincere
iurgium, iurgi, N., strife, quarrel
lis, litis, F., contention, strife
vultus, vultus, M., countenance, face
probus, -a, -um, good, virtuous, excellent
saeculum, saeculi, N., generation, age

Balthasar Jenichen (d. c. 1621),
Charity with Seven Children,
woodcut. Courtesy of A.L. Van Gendt
B.V. Blaricum.

Ubi Caritas

U*bi caritas* may be among the earliest Christian chants known, dating to the very beginnings of the religion's institutionalized worship. Historically, the earliest traces of hymnody go back to the second and third centuries when the celebration of the Lord's Supper was held weekly on the evening of the Lord's Day. In its earliest form the ritual celebration was closely linked with a love feast, or *agape,* a term taken form the Greek verb "to love", which was used in the early church to designate various forms of fraternal meals. The *agape* could be observed as an accompaniment to the Eucharist, or separate from it, serving as a symbol of Christ's love for mankind. The *agape,* or common meal, was accompanied by the recitation of prayers and singing. A letter of Pliny the Younger to the Emperor Trajan, written about 112 A.D., describes such a Christian fraternal meal. In the *New Oxford History of Music,* the chapter "Latin Chant before St. Gregory" by Monsignore Higini Anglès contains the observation ".....some chants have actually been preserved from the *agape,* such as 'Ubi caritas et amor', which might be taken as the beginning of Latin hymnody in Christian worship....." This citation gives *Ubi caritas* an incredible and breath-taking antiquity.

Further investigation beclouds the issue of authorship, as Father Connelly states that *Ubi caritas* can now be attributed to Rufinus of Aquilea, a fourth century monk, translator, and theological commentator. Elsewhere, although authorship is listed as unknown, the period of composition has been placed in Carolingian France, when, under Charlemagne, there was a rebirth of interest in the classics. Some of the odes of Horace and even portions of the *Aeneid* were set to music in notation form, though the notation remains indecipherable. The Carolingian court poets and musicians were equally prodigious in the production of religious lyrics, so it could be that a Frankish hand first wrote the beautiful Hymn of Charity.

By tradition *Ubi caritas* came to be associated with the Holy Thursday ritual of the washing of the feet, the *mandatum* service, so-called from the opening words of the first antiphon of the rite, *Mandatum novum* (a new commandment I give you). The ritual washing of the feet was common in the primitive church and was first mentioned as a liturgical rite in the canons of the seventeenth Synod of Toledo held in 694. The ritual was in use at the Monte Cassino monastery and elsewhere in Italy in the eleventh and twelfth centuries. By the eleventh century the practice had made its way to Rome where the papacy has continued the observance of the ritual washing on Holy Thursday. The ritual washing of the feet is an act of humility, a symbolic reference to baptism, and, above all, an affirmation of brotherly love as seen from the use of *Ubi caritas* as the accompanying hymn.

Albrect Dürer (1471-1528), *Christ Washing Peter's Feet*, woodcut. Courtesy of Dover Publications, Inc.

The verse employs lines of twelve or thirteen syllables with a division after the eighth syllable. Three verses are found in Connelly's *Hymns of the Roman Liturgy,* but the actual medieval hymn was longer. The choral setting of Duruflé is based on the first verse only. Although *Ubi caritas* may not have the great intrinsic value of some other Latin hymns, its moving simplicity has given it a lasting place through the centuries. From an early Christian *agape,* from the Frankish court of Charlemagne, from the great abbey of Monte Cassino where St. Benedict founded the Benedictine order, to the basilica of St. Peter's, the words of this beautiful Latin hymn have touched the hearts of the faithful. Even so, the words have inspired a twentieth century French composer to give new harmonies to the ancient Hymn of Charity.

Maurice Duruflé (1902-1986), born in Louviers, France, studied organ, harmony, and composition at the Paris Conservatoire where he earned numerous prizes for his organ compositions and playing. As an organ virtuoso he performed in Europe, Russia, and the United States. Duruflé's *Requiem,* which is his most frequently performed work, pre-miered in 1947. After the *Requiem* Duruflé did not publish again until 1960 when his four motets on Gregorian themes appeared, including *Ubi caritas.* While Duruflé wrote in the modern age of harmony and polyph-ony, in both the *Requiem* and the later motets, elements of plainchant can be heard. Whereas the monophonic chants of the early church sought to transfer the imagery of human prayer to a vocal setting, *Ubi caritas,* with its more complex vocal harmonies, preserves the tender expressiveness of the lyrics.

Gregorian rhythms have their preeminent interpretations in the recordings done by the monks of the Solesmes monastery, a Benedictine abbey of northwestern France. Solesmes has served as the center of contemporary revival of Gregorian chant. From the mid-nineteenth century on, the monks have revised, edited, and published chant books, usually with the active encouragement of the Vatican. The accumulated research, dating back over 100 years, has made the Solesmes scriptorium a mecca for students of medieval music who wish to consult its extensive manuscript collection. The chanting of the daily offices reflects current interpretations of medieval notation, a trend toward giving greater freedom and flexibility to Gregorian rhythm. This goal was expressed by Dom Joseph Pothier of Solesmes (1835-1923) in his preface to the series *Paléographie musicale:* "to raise Gregorian chant from the abject state into which it has fallen, to pursue the work of its restoration until complete justice is done, and it has recovered its full ancient beauty which rendered it so proper for divine worship." In point of fact, his goal has been achieved because the true performance standard for Gregorian chant is heard in the recordings of the monastic choir of Solesmes.

Ave Verum

TRANSLATION:

Ave verum Corpus natum
De Maria Virgine,
Vere passum, immolatum
In Cruce pro homine,
Cuius latus perforatum
Vero fluxit et sanguine,
Esto nobis praegustatum,
Mortis in examine.
O clemens, O pie,
O dulcis Jesu, Fili Mariae.

Hail, true Body, truly born
Of the Virgin Mary mild,
Truly offered, racked and torn,
On the Cross, for man defiled,
From whose love-pierced, sacred side
Flowed Thy true Blood's saving tide:
Be a foretaste sweet to me
In my death's great agony.
O Thou loving, gentle One,
Sweetest Jesus, Mary's son.

POULENC'S TEXT:

Ave verum corpus Christi,
natum ex Maria Virgine,
vere possum* immolatum
in cruce pro homine.

The Latin text and translation are from the
Hymns of the Breviary and Missal.

Possum, a misspelling of *passum,*
occurs in printed score.

VOCABULARY

nascor, nasci, natum, 3. to be born
patior, pati, passum, 3. to bear, to suffer
crux, crucis F., a tree, frame, wooden instrument of execution, cross
latus, lateris N., the side, flank
immolo, 1. to offer, to sacrifice
perforo, 1. to pierce through, to perforate
praegusto, 1. to taste beforehand
examen, examinis, N., a weighing, consideration, examination

AVE VERUM

This beautiful medieval hymn was written to be performed as part of the liturgy of the Roman Catholic Church, specifically after the consecration of the bread and wine, as the priest raises the host on high. "Hail the true body," the hymn begins, and the theme of truth, *verum*, of the opening is echoed in line 3, *vere*, truly, and again in line 6, *vero*, in truth.

The author of the poetry is usually listed as unknown, although several names appear in anthologies as possible authors. The *Historical Companion to Hymns Ancient and Modern* assigns the text to Pope Innocent V, who died in 1276, with a very noticeable question mark prefacing his authorship. Innocent V was the first Dominican to ascend to the papacy, although he occupied the post only for the first six months of 1276. Innocent had collaborated with Thomas Aquinas and Albertus Magnus in drafting the rules of studies for the Dominicans. Having a sound training in theology, Innocent wrote extensively on religious and ethical subjects, thereby earning a reputation as a man of learning, rather than a political activist. Innocent V was beatified in 1898.

The Reverend Matthew Britt in *The Hymns of the Breviary and Missal* assigns the hymn to Pope Innocent VI, whose papacy extended from 1352 to 1362, during the period known as the Babylonian Captivity when the papacy was removed to Avignon in France. Innocent, the fifth of the Avignon popes, served at a time when religion throughout Europe was facing challenges, this being the era of the Hundred Years' War and the ravages of the Black Death. Through his vigorous efforts at reform, Innocent corrected numerous abuses of the Papal Curia, but his resources were eventually dissipated in his wars to regain the Papal States as a step to the restoration of the papacy to Rome.

One early manuscript of *Ave verum* is from the Benedictine monastery of Reichenau in southwestern Germany. The manuscript, dating from the fourteenth century, bears the note, *Salutationem sequentem composuit Innocentius papa; haec oratio habet tres annos indulgentiarum a dom. papa Leone.* (Pope Innocent composed the following salutation; this prayer has three years of indulgences granted by Pope Leo.) More recently, the *Catholic Encyclopedia* discounts the probability that Innocent VI was the author since the text of *Ave verum* has been found in late thirteenth and early fourteenth century manuscripts. Furthermore, a comparison of the biographies of the two Innocents would incline the reader to favor Innocent V, the devout theologian and friend of Aquinas, rather than the later pope, known as a jurist, reformer, and diplomat.

In addition to the two Innocents, Thomas Aquinas himself, the great medieval philosopher and theologian, has been mentioned as a possible

Albrecht Dürer
(1471-1528),
*Christ on the Cross
with Three Angels,*
woodcut.
Courtesy of Dover
Publications, Inc.

45

author of the text. Aquinas, so revered for his piety and his learning that he was often referred to as the Angelic Doctor, lived in a century of intellectual fervor caused by the rediscovery of the writings of Aristotle. Within the scholastic movement, Aquinas worked to bring Aristotelian philosophy into harmony with Christian teaching. Perhaps because *Ave verum* is thematically linked to the reverence for the body of Christ, *Corpus Christi,* Aquinas is a logical source for the text. When, in 1264, Pope Urban IV instituted the feast of *Corpus Christi,* Aquinas was commissioned to write the hymns for the new feast day. His five eucharistic hymns are at the same time magnificent poetry and profound statements about Catholic theology. Aquinas' hymns for *Corpus Christi* are: *Lauda Sion salvatorem,* " O Sion, praise the Savior;" *Pange lingua gloriosi,* "Sing, my tongue, the Savior's glory;" *Sacris solemniis iuncta sint gaudia*, "Let joys be joined to our solemn feasts;" *Verbum supernum prodiens,* "The heavenly word proceeding forth;" *Adoro te devote, latens deitas,* "Hidden God, devoutly I adore Thee."

There are numerous variations in the wording of *Ave verum* from the various manuscript sources. One modern variation, however, an apparent misspelling, found its way into the printed music of Poulenc's motet, where, in the third line, the word *passum* is spelled *possum* and appears thus in the score. Although *Ave verum* is no longer found in the Breviary or Missal, it is frequently heard in concert performance in the popular motet setting of Mozart. Poulenc employs only the first four lines of the text in his modern motet. The verse is in trochaic tetrameter with rhyming at the end of the lines and some internal rhyme at the end of the caesura.

Francis Poulenc (1899-1963) was a Paris-born composer and pianist who produced piano, chamber and orchestral music, music for the stage, songs for solo voice, and choral music. In the field of French religious music of the twentieth century Poulenc shares supremacy with Olivier Messiaen. Poulenc's opera "Dialogues des Carmélites," one of three stage works he composed, has an international popularity. In the 1930's, Poulenc, after several personal crises, returned to the Roman Catholic faith of his childhood, and until his death he continued to produce religious choral music.

Composed in 1952, *Ave verum* was Poulenc's last motet and his shortest, and it is the only one of his motets written for a women's chorus. The music was commissioned by the Women's Chorus of Pittsburgh and it is dedicated to them. Poulenc composed eleven motets from the years 1938 to 1952, all employing Latin texts. The composer's musical treatment of the text follows the classical pronunciation of the Latin syllabic accent, with the exception of the word *cruce*, which is correctly accented on the first syllable, but receives second syllable stress, according to the melodic setting. The motet begins in the style of a canon, with the soprano voices introducing the theme which is, in turn, taken up by the second sopranos, and finally by the altos, wherafter the full chorus treatment continues. Poulenc's biographer, Keith W. Daniel, notes that *Ave verum* "contains some of Poulenc's most perfectly-fashioned choral writing."

Dulcis Amica

Dulcis amica, veni, veni, noctis
    solatia praestans!
Inter aves et enim nulla tibi
    similis.
Tu Philomela potes vocum
    discrimina mille, mille,
    mille, mille potes,
Varios ipsa referre modos.

Translation:

Sweet lady, come, come
    foremost comfort of the night!
For among all the birds,
    there is none like you.
You, Philomela, can mimic
    thousands of different voices.
You yourself can trill
    thousands of varying melodies.

Vocabulary

solatia/solatium, solatii N., help, consolation
praestans, praestantis, excellent, distinguished
discrimen, discriminis N., distinction, difference

The Birds, woodcut, from *Propriétaire des Choses*, Lyons, 1482. Courtesy of Houghton Mifflin Co.

Dulcis Amica

The volume of sacred music composed by Jacob Handl in his relatively brief lifetime (1550-1591) stands as a monument to this gifted Renaissance composer. (See *O admirabile commercium* for further biographical notes.) In the last three years of his life Handl also found time to compose one hundred Latin secular madrigals, a collection entitled *Harmoniarum moralium* (Moral Harmonies), commonly referred to simply as the *Moralia*. The *Moralia* were published in four volumes from 1589 to 1596, the last volume appearing after the composer's death. Allen Skei has turned his scholarly attention to the *Moralia*, as well as to Handl's sacred music, offering his observations in *The Musical Quarterly*.

The first book of the madrigals, printed in Prague, bears this Latin inscription on the title page:

> *Quatuor vocum Liber I. Harmoniarum Moralium quibus heroica, facetiae, naturalia, quotlibetica, tum facta fictaque poetica, &c. admixta sunt: nunc primum in lucem editus, Authore Iacobo Handl.* [For four voices, the first book of Moral Harmonies, to which are added things heroic, humorous, natural, quodlibets, as well as poetic facts and fictions, etc., now first published, the author being Jacob Handl.]

The quodlibets referred to in the title are well-known texts or melodies which appear in successive combinations, usually for a humorous effect, or as a showpiece for musical virtuosity. The term is from the Latin "what you please."

In his preface to the *Moralia* Handl justifies using his talents for something other than sacred composition, citing the urging of his young friends to "Drop your cares and enjoy life now and then." These friends implore him to descend from his choir loft to the marketplace, "*e Choro ad forum.*" It is very interesting that Handl gives his reasons for using Latin texts when there is a wealth of new secular music in the vernacular tongues of Italy, France and Germany. Referring to these vernacular songs Handl continues:

> All of us...would enjoy it if our ignorance of foreign tongues did not prevent us. I see that Latin is the queen of languages in this regard but that she is almost forsaken. It is to this most distinguished, richest language, which is at home everywhere, that I therefore now commit whatever I can elicit or derive from manners, the arts, or nature herself, whatever I can compose in a poetic style from sayings or facts or fictions variously mingled together.

In Handl's lifetime the most important post-classical source of texts was a sixteenth century anthology, *Carmina Proverbialia*, which had first been published in 1576 in Basel. The *Carmina* contained some complete poems, but consisted mainly of proverbs of one or two lines of text, which are arranged alphabetically from *Absurda* to *Vulgus*.

Handl's themes in the *Moralia* are as varied as the sources of his texts. Many seem to have a brief moral message for the listener, but others are purely for pleasure. Handl employs Dido's sad fate from book IV, beginning, *Dulces exuviae, dum fata Deusque sinebant...* (O relics of him, things dear to me while fate, while heaven allowed it...). In a totally different mode he composed a madrigal humorously titled *Quam gallina suum parit ovum* (How the hen lays her egg).

Skei speculates that Handl wrote the *Moralia* to be sung and heard by a rather well-educated audience. There were literary fraternities in Bohemia in the sixteenth century which were avid performers of the best polyphonic music of their times. Church choirs might have employed the *Moralia* when they sang at private gatherings and Handl did send copies of some of the madrigals to his clerical friends. Handl, as noted, championed the use of Latin for his texts and he was attentive to the rhythms and inflections of the

Latin in his musical settings. The madrigals allowed Handl a greater range for musical expression than did his sacred compositions, but it was Handl's sacred music which continued to be published and performed. The four-part *Moralia* were apparently never reprinted and there was only one reprinting of the madrigals for five or more voices. Skei states that after Handl, the Latin madrigal as a musical genre disappeared.

The madrigal *Dulcis amica* is based on a tale from Greek mythology, one of the "fictions" which Handl cites in his preface. The story of Philomela, from Book VI of Ovid's *Metamorphoses*, is a sad and bloody tale of passion and revenge. Tereus, a wealthy and influential king, weds Procne, the daughter of Pandion, king of Athens. Procne, homesick for her dear sister Philomela, sends Tereus to Athens to fetch her sister for a visit. Tereus,

enthralled by Philomela's charms, rapes his wife's sister, cuts out her tongue, and hides her away in a forest tower. When Procne learns of the crime, she rescues her sister Philomela and together they slaughter Procne's young son Itys, and serve him as dinner to the unknowing Tereus. When recognition comes, the king pursues Procne and Philomela and all three are transformed into birds: Procne, a swallow, Philomela, a nightingale, and Tereus, a hoopoe.

Pyramus and Thisbe, woodcut, from *Métamorphosé moralisé,* 1484. Courtesy of Constable & Co., Ltd.

51

Douglas Bush in *Mythology and the Renaissance Tradition in English Poetry* traces the story of Philomela through several interesting reworkings by medieval writers who doted on Ovid's work almost as much as on Vergil's. In an Old French poem *Philomena* the love story is elaborated into a much longer version, with added details of Philomela's charm and wit, along with other rhetorical flourishes. In another medieval retelling of Ovid, *Ovide moralisé*, from near the end of the thirteenth century, an entire treatise on morals and theology is heaped upon Ovid's tale. Bush outlines the medieval "moralized" version, which is in itself a metamorphosis of the classical verse.

> Pandion is God, who marries the soul, Progne, to the body, Tereus, in order that their offspring may replace the wicked angels who were cast out of heaven... The soul and body lived well together, and had a son Itys... But Progne longed to see her syster (the world and its pleasures), and sent Tereus over land and sea to obtain those earthly delights which God had granted to be used in moderation. The body, however, fixed all its thoughts upon these (Tereus' violation of Philomela), and hoarded them with avaricious care (the immuring of Philomela in the charge of an old woman). The soul forsakes the good for the evil life... and gives itself up to sin (the releasing of Philomela). The fruit of good life is destroyed (the murder of Itys). The soul flies to hell, the vile body becomes a hoopoe, and Philomela is changed into a nightingale.

Handl certainly did not have a Christian allegory in mind when he wrote *Dulcis amica,* nor was he caught up by the violent passions of Ovid's tale. He chose, instead, to be inspired by the nightingale, the most musically versatile of all birds, and to imitate, in his music, the song of the bird. In the madrigal, the refrain "Mille, mille, mille" is repeated with constantly varying pitch and melodic line, to mimic the sound of the nightingale.

Non Nobis, Domine

Latin Text:

Non nobis, Domine, non nobis,
    sed nomini tuo da gloriam.

Translation:

Not to us, O Lord, not to us, but to
    your name give glory.

David, die Psalmen singend Aus der Kobergerbibel, woodcut,
c. 1483. Courtesy of Verlag Friedrich Reinhardt, Basel.

Non Nobis, Domine

The text is from the Old Testament, Psalm 115, the first verse. The Book of Psalms, or Psalter, contains 150 religious poems which were brought together a few centuries before the beginning of the Christian era, having been composed over a long span of time, from the tenth to the fourth centuries B.C.. Although the entire collection is often referred to as the Psalms of David, the actual number which can be ascribed to the great shepherd king who died c. 962 B.C. is a matter of dispute in Biblical scholarship.

The word "psalm" derives, through the Latin, from a Greek word used to translate the Hebrew term for "song with stringed-instrument accompaniment." The ancient tradition in the Jewish temple rites of combining songs with instrumental music is recorded in various places in the Old Testament. The Psalter, or psalm collection, was adopted by the early Christians from the synagogue, and from the year 200 it became the paramount Christian prayer book. One of the Hebrew influences which the early church likewise adopted was the treatment of the psalm as a responsory. The responsorial form could be either that of a soloist singing a verse while the choir or congregation answered with a simple refrain, or with two singing groups doing the verses in alternation, that is antiphonally. Psalm singing became an integral part of the liturgy of the Mass and of the daily Offices of the Roman Church.

After the Reformation of the sixteenth century, the Protestant churches used metrical translations of the Psalms for congregational singing. In time psalm tunes became the source of some Protestant hymns, and in the German Lutheran tradition the singing of the psalms was the foundation of the development of the chorale. Thus, the long tradition of psalm singing from the Hebrew synagogue to the Roman Catholic mass, even to the Protestant hymn, has been man's attempt to praise God in word and song. The Latin text of Psalm 115 lies firmly within that long tradition, as St. Jerome's fourth century translation of the Book of Psalms brought the ancient Hebrew verse to the ears of generations of Christian faithful.

Although the translation of the psalm into Latin can be dated, there is not sufficient internal evidence to date the composition of Psalm 115 or the circumstances which inspired it. In the Septuagint version of the Old Testament, Psalms 114 and 115 are treated as one long poem of twenty-six verses. Both psalms belong to a group of psalms which were sung by the Jews at the conclusion of the Passover meal, the theme being the glorification of God and God's name. The complete first verse of the Psalm is: "Not unto us, O Lord, not unto us, but unto thy name give glory, for thy mercy, and for thy truth's sake."

As a literary curiosity, *Non Nobis* is mentioned in Shakespeare's *King Henry the Fifth,* in the fourth act, when, after the Battle of Agincourt, the king proclaims:

> Do we all holy rites;
> Let there be sung *Non Nobis* and *Te Deum.*
> The dead with charity enclosed in clay,
> We'll then to Calais; and to England then;
> Where ne'er from France arrived more happy men.

For his historical plays Shakespeare drew on the *Chronicles of England, Scotland, and Ireland,* compiled and first published in 1578 by Raphael Holinshed. The *Chronicles* describe Henry's victory at Agincourt:

> ...and gathering his armie togither , gaue thanks to
> almightie God for so happie a victorie, causing his prelats
> and chapleins to sing this psalme: In exitu Israel de
> Aegypto [114], and commanded euerie man to kneele
> downe on the ground at this verse: Non nobis Domine,

> non nobis, sed nomini tuo da gloriam. Which doone, he
> caused Te Deum, with certeine anthems to be soong,
> giuing laud and praise to God, without boasting of his
> owne force or anie humane power.

Non Nobis was composed by **William Byrd** (1543-1623), an Elizabethan musician whose name is preeminent in sixteenth century British
music. Indeed, the editors of the Oxford *Tudor Church Music* state,
"William Byrd is, in the opinion of many competent judges, the greatest
composer that this country has produced at any period of its history." He
was equally regarded for his prodigious talents by his contemporaries, one
of whom hailed Byrd as "Britannicae Musicae Parens."

Byrd's compositions were both religious and secular, both in Latin and
English, and he composed for solo voice as well as for chorus. In addition,
he composed instrumental pieces which rank Byrd as a pioneer of instrumental chamber music. Byrd himself considered his Latin music to be his
finest work. In 1575, during Byrd's lifetime, the very first volume of music
to Latin texts was published in England, *Cantiones, quae ab argumento
sacrae vocantur.* The book was dedicated to the queen who is praised for
her excellence "vel vocis elegantia, vel digitorum agilitate" (as much for the
elegance of her voice as for the agility of her fingers).

Because Byrd lived in the period of the infancy of the Anglican church,
he was called upon to compose a great body of English liturgical music for
the new church. Nevertheless, Byrd, a Roman Catholic, suffered person-
ally on numerous occasions from the Elizabethan persecutions of Catho-
lics; his favor at court, however, protected him from the worst excesses of
this persecution. After the composer's death, Byrd's Latin music was
eclipsed by his Anglican music until the late nineteenth century when there
was a revival of interest in Tudor music and Byrd's Latin music again
found an audience.

In the second volume of *Tudor Church Music* an interesting anecdote
is related concerning Byrd. It comes from a manuscript in the Christ

Church collections in which a footnote has been inserted into a text of Cicero's letters. In one of Cicero's letters to Atticus he writes:

> Britannici belli exitus expectatur: etiam illud iam cognitum est, neque argenti scrupulum esse ullum in ea insula, neque ullam spem praedae, nisi ex mancipiis, ex quibus nullos puto te literis aut musicae eruditos expectare. (The end of the Britannic war is awaited: for it has now been learned that there is not the smallest bit of silver on that island nor any hope of loot, unless it be from slaves; I think that you will find among them none trained in letters or music.)

The footnote states, "Unus Birdus omnes Anglos ab hoc convicio prosus liberat." (One man, Byrd, frees all the English completely from this insult.)

Byrd's compostion is in the form of a round, a term derived from the medieval Latin *rota* (wheel), although the more generic musical term "canon" could also be used to describe it. A round is meant to be performed by singers who each begin the melody at regular intervals, with the first voice completing a phrase, then the next voice entering, and so on. Historically the round dates back to the thirteenth or fourteenth century, maintaining its popularity through succeeding centuries. The old favorites "Frère Jacques" and the Latin "Dona Nobis Pacem" are just two familiar examples of rounds; more complex and musically challenging examples abound, many the work of well-known classical composers. This lovely round by Byrd serves as a reminder of how extensive the sounds of Latin music were in the age of Elizabeth and Shakespeare. William Byrd's long life of composing for England's two churches and for the court has given the musical world a treasury of Latin choral music. As the above-mentioned manuscript further notes:

> Birde, suos iactet si Musa Britanna clientes,
>   Signiferum turmis te creet illa suis.

> [O Byrd, if the British Muse were to boast of her minions,
> She would select you the standard-bearer for her troops.]

O Sacrum Convivium

LATIN TEXT:

O sacrum convivium!
In quo Christus sumitur:
recolitur memoria
passionis eius:
mens impletur gratia.

O sacrum convivium!
In quo Christus sumitur:
mens impletur gratia:
et futurae gloriae
nobis pignus datur.
Alleluia.

TRANSLATION:

O sacred communion! In which
the body of Christ is consumed:
the memory of his passion is
renewed: the mind is filled
with grace.

O sacred communion! In which
the body of Christ is consumed:
the mind is filled with grace: and
a pledge is given us of the glory
to come.

The translation is from the Argo recording
*O Sacrum Convivium, Modern French
Church Music.*

VOCABULARY

convivium, convivii N., banquet
sumo, -ere, sumpsi, sumptum, to take upon oneself, select, take
recolo, -ere, recolui, recultum, to resume, renew, call to mind
passio, passionis F., suffering, passion
pignus, pignoris N., pledge, token, assurance

O Sacrum Convivium

O *sacrum convivium* (O Holy Feast) is again a work of definite medieval origin, yet uncertain authorship. The text is found in several ancient breviaries, books containing the hymns and prayers which priests of the Western Church were accustomed to recite daily. The term *breviarium* may have come from the fact that the service book contained a shortened form of earlier Office Books. So long as religious communities remained as congregations or as monastic units, the various books needed by the priests and choirs could be extensive and inclusive, furnishing all the required readings for the liturgical year. The need for a portable breviary, however, became apparent in the thirteenth century with the appearance of the mendicant orders, notably the Franciscans, who did not reside in fixed religious communities. Breviaries were both numerous and varied; those of medieval England, France, and Germany number in the hundreds. As a consequence, a particular volume generally contains an identifying name: the Ambrosian Breviary of the Church of Milan, is one example.

In 1493, a York Breviary, used in the diocese of York, England, contained *O Sacrum Convivium* as an antiphon to be sung at the gospel on the festival of *Corpus Christi*. An antiphon is a musical addition to the reading of scripture which may be sung before or after the reading. The antiphon may be an original composition, or a quotation from scripture. An even earlier manuscript of *O sacrum convivium* is contained in a Sarum Processional in the British Museum, dating to c. 1390. The cathedral centers of the English rites furnished processional manuals which described and sometimes illustrated the proper vestments for the clergy, the role of the choir, plus complete texts of the appropriate scripture, hymns, and prayers. Neither the Sarum, which refers to the Cathedral of

Salisbury, nor the later York manuscript identifies an author for the text of
O sacrum convivium.

In 1953, the Roman Catholic Church published *The Pius X Hymnal*
as a tribute to the memory of Pius X, whose pontificate extended from
1903 to 1914. Pius X had worked to foster the study and improvement of
liturgical music, leading to the establishment in New York City of the
School of Liturgical Music which bears his name. *The Pius X Hymnal*
attributes *O sacrum convivium* to Saint Thomas Aquinas, who, it has
been pointed out, composed many hymns, particularly around the theme
of *Corpus Christi.* Whereas *The Pius X Hymnal* in printing the hymn
Ave Verum lists the authorship as "ascribed to Innocent VI," there is no
such qualification added to Aquinas' credit for *O sacrum convivium.* It
should be noted, however, that there is an ongoing scholarly controversy
about Aquinas' role in the entire office of the *Corpus Christi* liturgy,
although there is agreement that his commission from Pope Urban IV to
write the mass for the new feast day makes Aquinas the principal author of
this event.

Olivier Messiaen (1908–1992) was one of the leading composers of
twentieth century France. A child prodigy who began to compose at age
seven, he entered the Paris Conservatoire when he was eleven. When he
finished his studies he became principal organist at the church of La Trinité
in Paris and continued in this post for more than 40 years. As professor of
harmony at the Paris Conservatoire and visiting professor in Europe and
the United States, Messiaen has influenced musicians all over the world.

In a very brief examination of Messiaen's music, two facets stand out
as noteworthy. One was a fascination with the rhythms of ancient Greek
and medieval music, as well as with Hindu and oriental compositions. The
other was his lifelong passion for bird song which he transcribed in the
field. Messiaen traveled widely in France and abroad to observe bird song
which he wrote down on paper in musical notation, rather than relying on

a tape recorder. Interestingly, Roger Nichols, in his study of Messiaen, tells that while traveling in Japan, the French composer conversed with a Japanese ornithologist in Latin.

Messiaen composed the choral piece *O sacrum convivium* in 1937, shortly after he became professor at the École Normale de Musique in Paris. The war soon interrupted his teaching, however, for Messiaen found himself a prisoner of war during the years 1940 and 1941.

Throughout his musical career, Messiaen experimented widely with rhythms and harmonies, and in this choral work he has fused the medieval verse with a modern musical interpretation. The result is a hauntingly beautiful composition — modern, yet spiritually akin to the medieval friar who wrote the lines, whether that was Thomas Aquinas or one of his contemporaries. When hearing Messiaen's melody, *mens impletur gratia*, the mind is, indeed, filled with grace.

On the occasion of Messiaen's eightieth birthday, in December, 1988, Zubin Mehta conducted the New York Philharmonic in the composer's orchestral work "*Et exspecto resurrectionem mortuorum.*" In the *New Yorker* of January 16, 1989, the reviewer writes, "On a New York afternoon, one visited eternity — responded to Messiaen's sounding of terrors and glories beyond a simple unbeliever's ken." Here again the Latin title affirms that the ancient words speak a spiritual message to a modern composer.

Hans Sebald Beham (1500-1550),
The Savior, woodcut.
Courtesy of Hacker Art Books, Inc.

DIVERSOS DIVERSA IUVANT

LATIN TEXT:

Diversos diversa iuvant, non omnibus annis
   omnia conveniunt, res prius apta nocet.
exultat levitate puer, gravitate senectus,
   inter utrumque manens stat iuvenile decus.
hunc tacitum tristemque decet, fit clarior ille
   laetitia et linguae garrulitate suae.
cuncta trahit secum vertitque; volubile tempus,
   nec patitur certa currere quenque via.

TRANSLATION:

Different things please different people;
not all things are suited to all years.
That which before was fitting is harmful now.
The boy rejoices in nimbleness, the old man in dignity,
and between the two, youthful charm stands firm.
It befits one to be quiet and sad;
the other wins greater renown by his gaiety and quickness of tongue.
Time is changeable and does not allow anyone to run in a fixed course;
it pulls along and moves about all things with itself.

Translation is from Skei's edition of the *Moralia*.

VOCABULARY

decus, decoris N., distinction, honor, grace
garrulitas, garrulitatis F., foolish talk, chattering
volubilis, volubile, revolving, changeable, rapid

Diversos Diversa Iuvant

This madrigal comes from the *Moralia* of Jacob Handl, the source of *Dulcis amica* as well. Although Ovid's writing is widely employed for subject matter in the *Moralia*, Handl has also drawn on other classical Latin authors: four of the madrigals are taken from the *Aeneid*, one from Vergil's *Eclogues*; Catullus and Martial are also represented. The madrigal *Diversos diversa iuvant* is a verse of a later Roman poet, Maximianus, who left a limited poetic collection, mainly elegies written toward the close of his life. From personal references in the elegies, a few biographical details can be gleaned. Maximianus, a sixth century native of Etruria, of a noble family, was sent by the emperor as an emissary to Constantinople. A prodigious drinker and womanizer, he was rescued from one of his frequent romantic misadventures by his close personal friend Boethius. Because Maximianus wrote candidly about the pitfalls of love and bemoaned the infirmities of old age, he was a popular poet among medieval students.

There are no traces of Christian belief in Maximianus' verses, only a pervading mood of bitterness and despair for the human condition. Although he lived at the same time as Fortunatus, one of the luminaries of early Christian poetry, Maximianus belonged clearly to the dying Roman world. In *A History of Secular Latin Poetry in the Middle Ages*, Raby concludes, "Maximianus is, therefore, in some sort, the last of the Roman poets."

In the eight-voice motet *Diversos,* Handl has the upper voices sing of the nimbleness and charm of youth, while the lower voices respond with the dignity which is the delight of old age. The text is found in the *Elegiae*, i. 103-110.

Amo, Amas, I Love a Lass and Poculum Elevatum

Text:

Amo amas I love a Lass,
As a Cedar tall and slender,
Sweet Cowslips grace is her
  nom'tive Case,
and she's of the Feminine gender.

(Chorus) Rorum corum sunt divorum,
Harum scarum Divo,
Tag rag merry derry perriwig
  and hat band,
Hic hoc horum genitivo.

Can I decline a Nymph divine,
Her voice as a Flute is dulcis,
Her oculus bright her manus white,
And soft when I tacto her pulse is.
(Chorus)

Oh how bella my puella,
I'll kiss secula seculorum,
If I've luck Sir she's my Uxor,
O dies benedictorum.
(Chorus)

The Meeting of the Lovers, woodcut,
from the *Hypnerotomachia,* 1499.
Courtesy of Burt Franklin.

Latin Text:

Poculum, poculum elevatum
Quod nobis est pergratum.
Poculum, poculum elevatissimum
Quod nobis est pergratissimum.
Bibamus, bibamus, bibamus
Bibe totum extra, nil manet intra,
Bibe totum extra, nil manet intra.

Hoc est bonum in visceribus meis
Hoc est bonum in visceribus tuis
Et nos consequimur laudes tuas
O quam bonum est
O quam jucundum est
Poculis fraternis gaudere.
O quam bonum est
O quam jucundum est
Poculis fraternis gaudere.

Translation

Drinking-cup, drinking-cup, raised
  on high
That is so pleasing to us.
Drinking-cup, drinking-cup, raised
  higher still,
That is most pleasing of all.
Let us drink, drink, drink,
Drink it all up, so nothing is left,
Drink it all up, so nothing is left.

This is good in my insides
This is good in your insides
And we sing out your praises.
Oh, how good it is,
Oh, how delightful it is,
To enjoy good fellows' cups!
Oh, how good it is,
Oh, how delightful it is,
To enjoy good fellows' cups!

Vocabulary

poculum N., goblet
pergratus -a -um, very delightful
viscus, visceris N., entrails
jucundus -a -um, pleasant

Catchpenny Print,
eighteenth century engraving.
Courtesy of Hart Publishing Co.

65

Amo, Amas, I Love a Lass and Poculum Elevatum

These two songs come from a collection of music associated with an eighteenth century English gentlemen's musical club. The *Warren Collection*, from which the pieces are taken, was issued annually from 1762 until 1793. The sponsor of the *Collection* was "The Noblemen and Gentlemen's Catch Club of London." These high-born amateurs apparently represented a certain aristocratic standard of what was "good taste" in the England of George III, and they pursued their musical pastimes with the same sort of ardor usually associated with a gentleman's quest for honor.

The Catch Club was not the only English musical society of its time. Thomas Day in the *Musical Quarterly* has written of this period as a "Renaissance Revival" when England and possibly Italy were still delighting in the complex polyphony of Renaissance music. The London Academy of Ancient Music was founded in 1710 to study and perform in public concert the works of Palestrina, Lassus, Victoria and English Renaissance composers. From surviving programs of the Academy's concerts, Day reports that the

Albrecht Altdorfer (c. 1480-1538), *Loving Couple,* woodcut. Courtesy of Hacker Art Books, Inc.

program frequently concluded with William Byrd's canon, *Non nobis, Domine.* A companion organization, the Madrigal Society, another gentlemen's choral group, performed English and Italian madrigals.

The Renaissance Revival embraced not only the performance of ancient music, but also witnessed the efforts of several musicians to collect and publish rare old music. One of these collectors was Thomas Warren, who planned to issue a six volume anthology of Renaissance music, a project which he was not able to complete. Had he succeeded, it would have been a landmark work in music history.

Warren did succeed, however, in his post as secretary of the Catch Club, in publishing the catches and glees known as the *Warren Collection,* and in his dedication to the *Collection* he thanks the Catch Club. "By your benign influence the admired Compositions of the Fifteenth and Sixteenth Centuries have been restored, many of which are annexed to this collection.

The Catch Club, still in existence, first met at Almack's Tavern in 1761, at a time when young men were infused with the spirit of optimism which had accompanied the accession of young George III to the throne in 1760. By fostering mainly English music, including madrigals, catches, and anthems, they brought together composers, performers and patrons in the most congenial circumstances. This convivial setting was attractive to the eminent James Boswell who is quoted by the editor of the Warren collection, Emanuel Rubin:

> There is a musical society in London called the Catch Club
> ... There are many members, among them people of quality
> and fashion and also some of the best singers in England....
> They have a truly excellent collection [of songs]. The sub-
> jects are gay: they celebrate the pleasures of wine and love.
> The words are for the most part spirited and the accompa-
> nying tunes match them in liveliness. These songs... have
> really a very agreeable harmony. Lord Eglington [a personal
> acquaintance] is one of the most famous members of this
> society.... He sings in charming taste. He had the goodness

> to teach me some songs. When I return to England, I hope
> to learn more.... How many happy evenings have I passed
> at his house, singing.

Shortly after the Club's founding, the custom was introduced of awarding cash premiums for the best offerings of each year, both in a serious and in a cheerful vein. The prizes carried with them enormous prestige and had a great influence on the vocal compositions of the time.

The principal musical forms of the competition were the catch, the canon, and the glee. The catch employed the simultaneous manipulation of music and a literary composition, the latter often humorous, which offered a great challenge in achieving a successful combination of witty lyrics with complex vocalizing. One particularly witty catch, in the guise of an epitaph, is cited in the introduction to the *Collection:*

> Beneath in the Dust the mouldy old crust
> of Nell Batchelor lately was shoven,
> She was skill'd in the Arts of Pyes Custards and Tarts
> and knew ev'ry trick of the Oven,
> Having liv'd long enough she made her last Puff,
> a Puff by her Husband much prais'd,
> Now here she doth lye to make a dirt Pye
> in hopes that her Crust will be raised.

In the canon, a well-used musical formula, a single melody was imitated by successive voices: in essence, a round. It, too, offered a favorite way of displaying musical virtuosity. *Non nobis, Domine* is one of the Warren canons. The glee was the newest form, very English and very sentimental, and its popularity was certainly linked to the nationalism of the time. Although it was in the tradition of informal social music, the glee was designed to show off solo voices. The Catch Club did not have to rely solely on gifted amateurs for its performances because its membership also included professional musicians who were admitted on an honorary status and did not have to bear the financial burdens of full membership.

The lyrics of the *Warren Collection* treat chiefly the themes of love, loyalty and pleasure, which is very close in spirit to the themes of the medieval student songs. The poetry of their eighteenth century contemporaries, such as William Blake or Robert Burns, is not part of the Catch Club repertoire, but rather that of an earlier age which appealed to the Club's conservative tastes. Shakespeare appears nine times, as well as Milton and Thomas Gray, from whose "Elegy in a Country Churchyard" a single stanza, "Here rests his head...", is worked into a catch. There are a number of Latin texts, especially among the sacred canons, which is not surprising, since a gentleman's education was heavily weighted with the classics. References to Greek and Latin names and themes appear frequently among the titles.

In *Amo, amas* the macaronic form, which is a combination of Latin and the English vernacular, produces a delightful humor for those who have even an elementary knowledge of Latin grammar. The author of *Amo, amas* is unknown, but the puns and nonsense forms attest to his sense of the ridiculous in certain aspects of Latin syntax. In the introduction to the Warren Collection, Malcolm Nelson contributes the section on the poetry of the Collection. He finds *Amo, amas* superb, "A delicious series of indefatigably awful puns in dog-Latin." *Amo, amas* is found in volume 3 of the Warren Collection.

Poculum elevatum, from volume 2, is ascribed to Dr. Thomas Augustine Arne, a leading figure in English theatrical music of the mid-eighteenth century. Although he wrote abundantly in the religious mode, masses, oratorios, and so forth, Arne's genius was for lyric and theatrical music. Many of his operettas have classical themes, such as *Dido and Aeneas, The Judgement of Paris,* and *Oedipus, King of Thebes.* Since Arne was a professional musician, it is not surprising that the Warren Collection contains twenty-nine compositions from his pen. Arne attained the title of "Doctor" in 1750 when he was granted the degree of Doctor of Music at Oxford University.

O Vos Omnes

Latin Text:

O vos omnes
Qui transitis per viam
Attendite et videte
Si est dolor
Sicut dolor meus.

Translation: (King James)

Is it nothing to you,
All ye who pass by?
Behold, and see
If there be any sorrow
Like unto my sorrow....

Jeremiah Weeping for Jerusalem, woodcut, from *Speculum Humanae Salvationis.* Courtesy of University of California Press.

O Vos Omnes

The text is from the *Bible,* the Lamentations of Jeremiah, the first chapter, twelfth verse. The book of Lamentations is made up of five separate poems, each of which comprises one of the book's five chapters. The poems are elegies, or dirges, commemorating the destruction of Jerusalem by the Babylonians in 586 B.C. Chapters one through four are alphabetic acrostics of twenty-two stanzas, one for each letter of the Hebrew alphabet. This type of acrostic is found in other Old Testament books and reflects both a belief in the magical properties of the acrostic and the general aid to memorization which an acrostic presents. The poems of Lamentations are the first Hebrew poetry with a recognized metrical structure.

The tradition that Jeremiah was the author of the Lamentations was an ancient one. In the Hebrew Bible, however, Lamentations does not follow the Book of Jeremiah, that order being established later in the Septuagint version. Attribution of the Lamentations to Jeremiah arose, understandably, because the poems must have been written by someone who, like Jeremiah, experienced the siege of Jerusalem and the miseries which followed its fall. Recent Biblical scholarship, however, casts doubt on Jeremiah's authorship, suggesting that there were instead several authors writing on a common theme. The poems are poignant expressions of grief at the tragic destruction of the city of Jerusalem. The opening lines of chapter 1, from which the text of *O vos omnes* is taken, express this deep sense of loss: "How doth the city sit solitary, that was full of people! how is she become as a widow! she that was great among the nations, and a princess among the provinces, how is she become tributary!"

Portions of the Lamentations are appointed for use throughout the church year: *O vos omnes* has a place on the September 15 Feast of the Seven Sorrows of the Blessed Mary, and during the Feast of the Sacred Heart of Jesus. Primarily, however, *O vos omnes,* with its overall theme of sorrow, is assigned to the season of Holy Week, which was the intent of the present composer, Pablo Casals.

Pablo Casals (1876-1973) was a Spanish cellist, composer, conductor and pianist whose long and illustrious international career brought about a new appreciation for the cello and its repertory. The son of musical parents, Casals was trained on the piano, organ and violin before he undertook cello studies at the age of eleven. His student years took him to Madrid, Brussels, and Paris from where he returned to Barcelona to teach and perform.

With a group of fellow Barcelona musicians, in 1919, Casals organized the Orquestra Pau Casals, using the Catalan spelling of his first name rather than the Castilian Pablo. The orchestra played in cities throughout Europe, and Casals' reputation as a conductor soon rivaled that of his reputation as a performer.

When, in 1931, the Spanish people voted for a republican form of government, King Alfonso XIII abdicated and fled to France. Within hours after the abdication, Catalonia proclaimed itself an autonomous republic. That night, in Barcelona, Casals conducted Beethoven's Ninth Symphony to an emotional audience, and following the performance the new head of the Catalonian government remarked to Casals, "Our republic has come in to the accompaniment of the 'Hymn of Brotherhood.'"

By 1936 Spain was seething with political turmoil. In mid-summer Casals was rehearsing his orchestra for a performance of Beethoven's Ninth when a government messenger interrupted the rehearsal with the announcement that a state of emergency had been declared, the concert canceled, and the orchestra was to be disbanded. The musicians tearfully completed the rehearsal, then left as the maestro proclaimed, "When our city and our country are once more at peace, we shall play the Ninth Symphony again."

The ensuing civil war and consequent Franco dictatorship forced Casals to take up residence on the French side of the Spanish border. He gave concerts during World War II in France to aid the Red Cross and his fellow Catalan refugees. In late 1945, after concerts in London and Paris, Casals stunned the musical community by announcing that he would give no more concerts until Spain was once again a free country. The musical silence was broken when, in 1950, Casals agreed to take part in a festival observance of the two hundredth anniversary of Bach's death which was organized to take place in Prades, the village of his exile. For the Bach festival, the little French village of Prades became the musical center of the world as musicians gathered from distant cities to hear the revered master cellist play his beloved Bach.

In his exile Casals never forgot the cause of a free Spain, a cause which moved him to correspond with various heads of government. President John F. Kennedy responded with an invitation to play at the White House on November 13, 1961. Casals accepted on the condition that he be allowed a private conversation with the President on the subject of world peace. When the eighty-five year old Casals played that evening in the East Room, the audience of political and musical dignitaries felt that they had witnessed the musical experience of a lifetime.

In addition to his long career as performer, teacher, and conductor, Casals also composed extensively, although most of his musical creations were not published during his lifetime. His sacred compositions were exceptions, for many were performed by the monks of the monastery of Montserrat, located near Barcelona. Casals was a frequent visitor at the monastery, which is a celebrated shrine of Our Lady of Montserrat, the patron saint of Catalonia, Casals' native province. Historically, religious music has been an important part of the monastery life of Montserrat; the troubadours of the Middle Ages celebrated Montserrat in song as the hiding place of the Holy Grail. From medieval to modern times Montserrat has produced eminent musicians and musical scholars. In his book of reflections, *Joys and Sorrows,* Casals wrote, "Over the years I have dedicated my religious compositions to the monastery. I have refrained from the publication of almost all my other works. The monks of Montserrat, however, have published my religious music. They sing my Masses regularly and my Rosary every day...."

The date of Casals' composition of *O vos omnes* is listed as 1932, although it is not known if Casals was in residence at Montserrat monastery when he composed it, as he was for other religious pieces of this same period. If there was a specific personal loss which led Casals to the Lamentations it could have been the death of his mother the previous year or the loss of his close friend, the Dutch composer Julius Rontgen. On the other hand, he may have been influenced by a general malaise as he observed the new Republican government's anti-clerical stance, its repression of the church, including the closing of all Roman Catholic schools. Casals first published *O vos omnes* for male chorus, then later for mixed chorus. In his religious music Casals reveals the same depth of feeling that he brought to his cello performances, his conducting, as well as to his patriotic and political causes. Through the medium of this great master's music, the modern listener is reunited with the sorrow of the Biblical Jeremiah, in the Latin translation of the Hebrew. The succinctness of the Latin verse has an eloquence that defies the translator's pen; it goes directly to the heart.

BIBLIOGRAPHY

Adey, Lionel. *Hymns and the Christian Myth.*
University of British Columbia Press, Vancouver, 1986.

The Age of Humanism, 1540-1630. Vol. 4 of *New Oxford History of Music.* Oxford University Press, London, 1968.

Allen, Philip Schuyler. *Medieval Latin Lyrics.*
The University of Chicago Press, Chicago, 1931.

————— *The Romanesque Lyric.*
The University of North Carolina Press, Chapel Hill, 1928.

Backhouse, Janet. *Books of Hours.* The British Library, London, 1985.

Barker, John W. *The Use of Music and Recordings for Teaching About the Middle Ages.* Medieval Institute Publications, Kalamazoo, 1988.

Beare, William. *Latin Verse and European Song.*
Methuen & Co., Ltd., London, 1957.

Benedictines of Solesmes, eds. *The Liber Usualis with Introduction and Rubrics in English.* Desclé and Co., Tournai, Belgium, 1947.

Britt, the Rev. Matthew, O. S. B., ed. *The Hymns of the Breviary and Missal.* Benziger Brothers, New York, 1922.

Brittain, Frederick. *The Medieval Latin and Romance Lyric to A. D. 1300.* Cambridge University Press, Cambridge, 1951.

Burns, Edward. *The Chester Mystery Cycle, A New Staging Text.*
Liverpool University Press, Liverpool, 1987.

Bush, Douglas. *Mythology and the Renaissance Tradition in English Poetry.* W. W. Norton and Company, Inc., New York, 1963.

Cattin, Giulio. *Music of the Middle Ages.* Vol. 1. Translated by Steven Botterill. Cambridge University Press, Cambridge, 1984.

Chambers, E. K. *The Medieval Stage.* 2 vols. Oxford University Press, Oxford, 1925.

Connelly, the Rev. Joseph, M.A. *Hymns of the Roman Liturgy.* The Newman Press, Westminister, Maryland, 1957.

Craig, Hardin. *English Religious Drama of the Middle Ages.* Clarendon Press, Oxford, 1955.

Davidson, Archibald T. and Apel, Willi. *Historical Anthology of Music.* Harvard University Press, Cambridge, Massachusetts, 1950.

Day, Thomas. "A Renaissance Revival in Eighteenth-Century England." *The Musical Quarterly* 57: 575-592.

DeAngelis, the Rev. Michel, C.R.M., PhD. *The Correct Pronunciation of Latin According to Roman Usage.* St. Gregory Guild, Inc., Philadelphia, 1937.

Dearmer, Percy, Williams, R. Vaughan, and Shaw, Martin, eds. *The Oxford Book of Carols.* Oxford University Press, London, 1928.

Douglas, Winfred. *Church Music in History and Practice.* Charles Scribner's and Sons, New York, 1962.

Draves, Guido Maria and Blume, Clemens, eds. *Analecta hymnica medii aevi.* 55 vols. Fues et al., Leipzig, 1886-1922.

Dronke, Peter. *The Medieval Lyric.* Hutchison & Co., London, 1978.

——— *Women Writers of the Middle Ages.* Cambridge University Press, Cambridge, 1984.

Duncan, Edmonstoune. *The Story of the Carol.* Walter Scott Publishing Co., London, 1911.

Dutka, JoAnna. *Music in the English Mystery Plays.*
Medieval Institute Publications, Kalamazoo, 1980.

Ebensberger, Gary Lee. *The Motets of Francis Poulenc.*
The University of Texas at Austin, D.M.A., 1970,
University Microfilms, Ann Arbor, Michigan.

Faculty of the Pius Tenth School of Liturgical Music, eds.
The Pius X Hymnal. McLaughlin and Reilly Co., Boston, 1953.

Fallows, David. *Dufay.* J. M. Dent and Sons, Ltd., London, 1982.

Forsee, Aylesa. *Pablo Casals, Cellist for Freedom.*
Thomas Y. Crowell Company, New York, 1965.

Frost, Maurice, ed. *Historical Companion to Hymns Ancient
and Modern.* William Clowes and Sons, Ltd., London, 1962.

The Golden Age of Dutch Manuscript Painting. Catalogue of Pierpont
Morgan Library Exhibition, with intro. by James H. Marrow.
George Braziller, Inc., New York, 1990.

Greene, Henry Copley. "Song of the Ass." *Speculum* 6
(1931): 534-549.

Greene, Richard Leighton. *The Early English Carols.* 2nd ed.,
Clarendon Press, Oxford, 1977.

Harrington, K. P. *Medieval Latin.* University of Chicago Press,
Chicago, 1962.

Holinshed, Raphael. *Chronicles of England, Scotland, and Ireland.*
6 vols. AMS Press Inc., New York, 1965.

Hoppin, Richard H. *Medieval Music.* W. W. Norton and Company Inc.,
New York, 1978.

Hughes, Andrew. *Medieval Manuscripts for Mass and Office: A Guide to their Organizaion and Terminology*. University of Toronto Press, Toronto, 1982.

————*Medieval Music, the Sixth Art*. University of Toronto, Toronto, 1974.

————*Style and Symbol, Medieval Music: 800-1453*. The Institute of Medieval Music, Ottawa, Canada, 1989.

Hughes, Dom Anselm, ed. *Early Medieval Music Up to 1300*. Oxford University Press, London, 1954.

Hymns Ancient and Modern Revised. William Clowes and Sons, Ltd., London, 1950.

The Interpreter's Bible. Abingdon Press, New York, 1956.

Jeffers, Ron, ed. *Translations and Annotations of Choral Repertoire*. Vol. 1: *Sacred Latin Texts*. earthsongs, Corvallis, OR, 1988.

Johnson, Robert Sherlow. *Messiaen*. University of California Press, Berkeley, 1975.

Joys and Sorrows, Reflections by Pablo Casals as told to Albert E. Kahn. Simon and Schuster, New York, 1970.

Julian, John, D.D., ed. *A Dictionary of Hymnology*. 2 vols. Dover Publications, Inc., New York, 1892, rev. 1957.

La Rue, Jan, ed. *Aspects of Medieval and Renaissance Music: A Birthday Offering to Gustave Reese*. W. W. Norton, New York, 1966.

Lindsay, Jack. *Song of a Falling World*. Andrew Dakers Ltd., London, 1948.

Lumiasky, R. M. and Mills, David. *The Chester Mystery Cycle*. University of North Carolina Press, Chapel Hill, 1983.

MacLean, Sally-Beth. *Chester Art*. Medieval Institute Publications, Kalamazoo, 1982.

Messenger, Ruth Ellis. *The Medieval Latin Hymn*. Capitol Press, Washington, D.C., 1953.

Nemmers, Erwin Esser. *Twenty Centuries of Catholic Church Music*. Greenwood Press, Westport, CT, 1949.

New Catholic Encyclopedia. McGraw Hill Book Company, New York, 1967.

Nichols, Roger. *Messiaen, Oxford Studies of Composers*. Oxford University Press, London, 1975.

Ninde, Edward S., D.D. *Nineteen Centuries of Christian Song*. Fleming H. Revell Company, New York, 1938.

Overath, Johannes, ed. *Sacred Music and Liturgy Reform After Vatican II*. Consociato Internationalis Musicae Sacrae, Rome, 1969.

Pierik, Marie. *The Song of the Church*. Longmans, Green and Co., New York, 1947.

Raby F. J. E. *A History of Christian Latin Poetry from the Beginnings to the Close of the Middle Ages*. 3 vols. 2nd. ed., Clarendon Press, Oxford, 1953.

——— *A History of Secular Latin Poetry in the Middle Ages*. 2 vols. 2nd. ed., Clarendon Press, Oxford, 1957.

Reese, Gustave. *Music in the Middle Ages*. W. W. Norton and Co., New York, 1940.

Richards, Jeffrey. *Consul of God, The Life and Times of Gregory the Great*. Routledge Kegan Paul, Ltd., London, 1980.

Routley, Erik. *The English Carol*. Herbert Jenkins Limited, London, 1958.

Sadie, Stanley, ed. *The New Grove Dictionary of Music and Musicians.* Macmillan Publishers, Ltd., London, 1980.

Schmitt, Francis P. *Church Music Transgressed.* The Seabury Press, New York, 1977.

Seay, Albert. *Music in the Medieval World.* Prentice-Hall, Inc., Englewood Cliffs, New Jersey, 1965.

Sebesta, Judith Lynn. *Carl Orff, Carmina Burana, Cantiones Profanae.* Bolchazy-Carducci, Chicago, 1985.

Skei, Allen B. "Jacob Handl's Moralia." *The Musical Quarterly* 52, (October 1966): 431-447.

——————— "Jacob Handl's Polychordal Music." *Music Review* 29, (1968): 81-95.

——————— ed., *The Moralia of 1596, Part I.* A R Editions, Inc., Madison, 1970.

Smith, H. Augustine. *Lyric Religion, the Romance of Immortal Hymns.* Fleming H. Revell Co., New York, 1931.

Smith J. A. "The Ancient Synagogue, The Early Church and Singing." *Music and Letters* 65 (January 1984): 1-16.

Spitzmuller, Henri. *Carmina sacra medii aevi: Poésie latine chrétienne du moyen âge: II-XV siècle.* Bibliothèque européenne, Bruges, Desclée de Brouwer, 1971.

Stevens, Denis, ed. *The Treasury of English Church Music.* 5 vols. Blandford Press, London, 1965.

Stevens, John, ed. *Early Tudor Songs and Carols.* Vol. 36 of *Musica Britannica, A National Collection of Music.* Stainer and Bell, Ltd., London, 1975.

———— *Words and Music in the Middle Ages: Song, Narrative, Dance and Drama.* Cambridge University Press, Cambridge, 1986.

Symonds, John Addington. *Wine, Women, and Song, Medieval Latin Student Songs Now First Translated into Verse.* Cooper Square Publishers, Inc., New York, 1966.

Szövérffy, Joseph. *A Concise History of Medieval Hymnody.* Classical Folia Editions, Leyden, 1985.

Tudor Church Music. Vol. 2. Oxford University Press, London, 1922.

Waddell, Helen. *Medieval Latin Lyrics.* Barnes and Noble, New York, 1966.

———— *More Latin Lyrics from Virgil to Milton.* Norton, New York, 1977.

———— *The Wandering Scholars.* Barnes and Noble, New York, 1966.

Warren, Thomas Edmond, ed. *A Collection of Catches, Canons and Glees.* 4 vols. Mellifont Press, Inc., Wilmington Delaware, 1970.

Whicher, George F. *The Goliard Poets, Medieval Latin Songs and Satires.* New Directions Publishing Corporation, New York, 1949.

Wieck, Roger S. *Time Sanctified, The Book of Hours in Medieval Art.* George Branziller, Inc., New York, 1988.

Wilhelm, James. J. ed. *Medieval Song, An Anthology of Hymns and Lyrics.* E. P. Dutton and Co., New York, 1971.

Wilkins, Nigel. *Music in the Age of Chaucer*. Boydell Press Ltd., Woodbridge, Suffolk, 1979.

Wright, F. A. and Sinclair, T. A. *A History of Later Latin Literature*. The Macmillan Company, New York, 1931.

Young, Karl. *The Drama of the Medieval Church*. 2 vols. Clarendon Press, Oxford, 1933.

Zeydel, Edwin. *Vagabond Verse, Secular Latin Poems of the Middle Ages*. Wayne State University Press, Detroit, 1966.

ACKNOWLEDGEMENTS

Translations

"The Virgin's Cradle Hymn" from *The Complete Poetical Works of Samuel Taylor Coleridge.* Vol. 1. Oxford University Press, 1957, and from *The Notebooks of Samuel Taylor Coleridge,* ed. by Kathleen Coburn. Vol. 1. Pantheon Books, Inc., 1957.

"Orientis Partibus" from *Speculum* 6 (1931).

"Mirabile Mysterium" from *Translations and Annotations of Choral Repertoire. Vol. 1: Sacred Latin Texts.* earthsongs, 1988.

"Ave Regina" and "Ubi Caritas" from the Rev. Joseph Connelly's *Hymns of the Roman Liturgy.* The Newman Press, 1957.

"Ave Verum" from *The Hymns of the Roman Breviary and Missal.* Benzinger Publishing Company, 1922.

"O Sacrum Convivium" from Argo Recording *Modern French Church Music.*

"Diversos Diversa Iuvant" from *The Moralia of 1596,* ed. by Allen B. Skei. Part 1 of *Recent Researches in the Music of the Renaissance.* Vol. 7. A-R Editions, Inc., 1970.

Illustrations

Abaris Books, Inc. Pleasantville, NY. *The German Single-Leaf Woodcut: 1600-1700,* ed. by Dorothy Alexander.

A. L. Van Gendt B.V. Amsterdam, The Netherlands. F. W. H. Hollstein's *German Engravings, Etchings and Woodcuts ca. 1400-1700.* Vols. 7 and 15.

Burt Franklin Publishers. New York, NY. Alfred W. Pollard's
    Italian Book Illustrations.

Constable Co., Ltd. London, England. Arthur M. Hind's
    An Introduction to a History of Woodcut.

Dick Sutphen Studio. Minneapolis, MN.
    Old Engravings and Illustrations. Vol. 1.

Dover Publications. New York, NY. *The Complete Woodcuts of
    Albrecht Durer,* ed. by Dr. Willi Kurth.

Friedrich Reinhardt Verlag. Basel, Switzerland.
    Die Illustration der Lutherbibel 1522-1700.

Hacker Art Books, Inc. New York, NY. Max Geisburg's
    The German Single-Leaf Woodcut: 1500-1550.

Hart Publishing Co., Inc. New York, NY. *Hart Picture Archives,
    Humor, Wit and Fantasy*.

Oxford University Press. New York, NY. Edward Hodnett's
    English Woodcuts 1480-1535.

The University of California Press. Berkeley, CA. Adrian Wilson and
    Joyce Lancaster Wilson's *A Medieval Mirror*.

Music Sources:

"Virgin's Cradle Hymn"   Edmond Rubbra
    Oxford University Press, Inc.
    200 Madison Ave.
    New York, NY 10016
    Oxford Choral Song #706, © 1954.

"Song of the Nuns of Chester"   Anonymous
    Oxford University Press, Inc.
    The Oxford Book of Carols
    Arr. by John Parkinson, © 1964.

"Orientis Partibus"   Anonymous
    Oxford University Press, Inc.
    Now Make We Mirth, © 1968.

"Mirabile Mysterium"   Jacob Handl
    E. C. Schirmer Music Co.
    112 South St.
    Boston, MA 02111
    E.C.S. #2214, © 1971.

"O Admirabile Commercium"   Jacob Handl
    Mercury Music Corp.
    Theodore Presser Co.
    Presser Place
    Bryn Mawr, PA 19010
    For 8 voices
    Ed. by Ernest White, © 1946.

"Ave Regina"   Guillaume Dufay
    Mercury Music Corp.
    Motet for 3 part chorus, © 1949.

"Ave Generosa"   Hildegard of Bingen
    Antico Edition
    P.O. Box 1
    Moretonhampstead, Newton Abbot
    Devon TQ13 8UA
    England
    Sequences and Hymns of Hildegard of Bingen
    Ed. by Christopher Page, © 1982.

"Hodie Christus Natus Est"   Francis Poulenc
    Editions Salabert
    G. Schirmer, Inc.
    225 Park Avenue South
    New York, NY 10003
    E.A.S. 16762, © 1962.

"Ubi Caritas"   Maurice Duruflé
   Durand Cie.
   21, Rue Vernet
   Paris, France 75008
   Pour 4 voix mixtes, © 1960.

"Ave Verum"   Francis Poulenc
   Editions Salabert
   G. Schirmer Inc.
   Motet à 3 voix de femmes
   © 1952 by Rouart-Lerolle et Cie.

"Dulcis Amica"   Jacob Handl
   Roger Dean Publishing Co.
   The Lorenz Corp.
   501 East Third St.
   P.O. Box 802
   Dayton, OH 45401-0802
   CA-103, ed. by P. D. Crabtree, © 1974.

"Non Nobis Domine"   William Bryd
   Musikverlag zum Pelikan
   Zurich, Switzerland
   #98 in *121 Canons zum Singen und
   spielen auf allerlei instrumentum*
   Ed. Edmund A. Cykler and Egon Kraus, © 1965.

"O Sacrum Convivium"   Olivier Messiaen
   Durand et Cie.
   Motet pour choeur à 4 voix mixtes, © 1937.

"Diversos Diversa Iuvant"   Jacob Handl
   A-R Editions, Inc.
   801 Deming Way
   Madison, WI 53717
   The Moralia of 1596, Part I
   Ed. by Allen B. Skei in
   *Recent Researches in the Music
   of the Renaissance,* vol. 8, 1970.

"Amo, Amas" and "Poculum Elevatum"   Anon. / Thomas Arne
    Mellifont Press, Inc.
    1508 Pennsylvania Ave.
    Wilmington, DE 19806
    U.S.A. Distributors
    Irish University Press, Inc.
    2 Holland Ave.
    White Plains, NY 10603
    A Collection of Catches, Canons and Glees, 4 vols.
    Ed. by Thomas Edmund Warren, 1970.
    "Amo" in vol. 3, "Poculum" in vol. 2.

"O Vos Omnes"   Pablo Casals
    Tetra/Continuo Music Group, Inc.
    c/o Mr. Robert J. Bregman
    960 Park Avenue/Apt. 10-E
    New York, NY 10028
    TC 128, © 1965.

Cynthia Ousley Kaldis, a native of Freeport, Illinois, received her undergraduate training at Oberlin College and the University of Wisconsin and completed a master's degree in education at Ohio University. She has taught Latin at Brookfield High School in Brookfield, Wisconsin, and at the American Community School in Athens, Greece. From 1974 to 1998 she taught both Latin and reading at Alexander High School in Albany, Ohio. She hopes that through this book, "some Latin students here and there may have their eyes and ears opened to the beauty of Latin choral music."

The Legend Lives Forever in Latin (Elvis Songs in Latin)
Jukka Ammondt

Sing along with Dr. Ammondt as he croons favorite Elvis ballads, including "Love Me Tender" *("Tenere me ama")* and "It's Now Or Never" *("Nunc Hic Aut Numquam")*. The CD booklet contains lyrics to all the songs, in both English and Latin.

CD with dual-language libretto
(1995) Order # 62002

Latine Cantemus: Cantica Popularia Latine Reddita
Franz Schlosser

This illustrated edition features sixty new Latin translations of popular songs, including nursery rhymes, chanties, folk songs, spirituals, and Christmas carols. Also included are three appendices of traditional Latin favorites, Christmas songs, and well-known Gregorian chants.

Illus., vii + 135 pp. (1996)
Paperback, ISBN 0-86516-315-4

Schola Cantans
Composed by Jan Novák
Sung by Voces Latinae

A cassette with musical arrangement of **Catullus, Horace, Caesar, Carmina Burana, Martial, Phaedrus.** Cassette is accompanied by a libretto with original Latin text and English translation on facing pages. Music score also available.

Cassette: 19 pp. (1998), ISBN 0-86516-357-X
Music Score: 46 pp. (1998), ISBN 0-86516-358-8
Cassette and Music Score Set: (1998), ISBN 0-86516-404-5

Bolchazy-Carducci Publishers, Inc.
http://www.bolchazy.com

Carmina Burana

by Judith Sebesta

CARL ORFF
CARMINA BURANA
CANTIONES PROFANAE

ORIGINAL TEXT WITH INTRODUCTION, FACING VOCABULARIES,
STUDY MATERIALS AND TRANSLATION
BY
JUDITH LYNN SEBESTA

The 24 "cantiones profanae" from the Middle Ages that were set to music by Carl Orff in 1937 are explored in fascinating detail in the *Carmina Burana* by Judith Sebesta. The poems are offered in their original Latin, with English translations by Jeffery M. Duban.

This book serves as the libretto for any of the numerous recordings of "Carmina Burana" and helps the listener to achieve a better understanding of and greater appreciation for the music.

Carmina Burana is a unique, stimulating book that will be welcomed by students, teachers and scholars of music, history, and language.

This edition includes:
+ Religious/Political Analyses
+ "Carmina Burana" Discography
+ Biography of Carl Orff
+ Extensive Notes & Vocabulary
+ Bibliography
+ Illustrations: Medieval & Contemporary

"...attractive, convenient, easy to use, lively and inexpensive.... an admirable project."
— **Peter L. Reid,** *NEC Newletter*

"This would be an excellent investment for the school library of stockroom."
— **The Joint Association of Classical Teachers**

Illus., 165 pp. (1937, Enhanced reprint 1996)
Paperback, ISBN 0-86516-268-9

Bolchazy-Carducci Publishers, Inc.
orders@bolchazy.com

New World Music
in
LATIN

Baroque Music from the Bolivian Rainforest

CD with
dual-language
libretto

Order #BB10

ROME'S GOLDEN POETS

Performed by the St. Louis Chamber Chorus under the direction of Philip Barnes

Co-published by the St. Louis Chamber Chorus
and Bolchazy-Carducci Publishers, Inc.

With its chronological, cultural, and ethnic diversity of composers, this CD recording testifies to the timeless power of the Golden Age of Roman poetry. Selections from Catullus, Vergil, and Horace are performed by the St. Louis Chamber Chorus under the direction of Philip Barnes.

Horace
Felices Ter/Johann Walther/(1496–1570)
Felices Ter (from Six Odes of Horace)/Randall Thompson/(1899–1984)
Iustum et Tenacem/Zoltán Kodály/(1882–1967)
Montium Custos (from Six Odes of Horace)/Randall Thompson
O Venus/Peter Cornelius/(1824–1874)
Vitas Hinnuleo (from Six Odes of Horace)/Randall Thompson
Rectius Vives/Zoltán Kodály
Oderunt Hilarem Tristes/Jacob Handl
O Fons Bandusiae (from Six Odes of Horace)/Randall Thompson/(1899–1984)
Principibus Placuisse Viris/Jacob Handl
In Honorem Vitæ/Antonín Tucapsky/(b. 1928)
    Ne forte credas; Iam satis; Nunc est bibendum; Eheu, fugaces; Tu ne quæsieris
Old Horatius Had A Farm/Z. Randall Stroope

Catullus
Odi Et Amo/Jacob Handl/(1550–1591)
Passer Mortuus Est/Gian-Francesco Malipiero/(1882–1973)

Vergil
Fama, Malum Qua Non Aliud Velocius Ullum/Josquin Des Pres/(c. 1455–1521)
Dulces Exuviæ/Josquin Des Pres
Dulces Exuviæ/Adrian Willært/(c. 1490–1562)
At Trepida et Cœptis Immanibus Effera Dido/Jacob Arcadelt/(c. 1505–c. 1567)
Oráculo/José Antônio de Almeida Prado/(b. 1943)
Dulces Exuviæ/Jacob Handl

(1999) Limited edition CD, ISBN 0-86516-474-6

Bolchazy-Carducci Publishers, Inc.
http://www.bolchazy.com

Vergil's *Dido* and *Mimus Magicus*

Composed by
Jan Novák

Conducted by
Rafael Kubelik

Performed by
the **Symphony Orchestra** of the ***Bayerischer Rundfunk*** (Germany)

Composer Jan Novák's haunting choral rendition of Vergil's ancient poetry commences with the voice of Dido the queen, foreshadowing a tragic tale of love and duty. Widely acclaimed in Europe, Novak's "Dido and Mimus Magicus" conducted by Rafael Kubelik is now available to American audiences in a CD recording with a 3-language libretto.

In his large-scale oratorio recounting the fateful events of the life of Dido, Jan Novák (1921–1984) responded to Vergil's highly charged verses with music of an exceptionally dramatic nature. Rafael Kubelik leads the forces of the Bayerischer Rundfunk in a compelling and well recorded performance that captures the pathos of Novák's score. The highlight of the performance is Marilyn Schmiege's superb interpretation of the very demanding role of Dido. A release of special merit that deserves a place in any collection of twentieth-century music and an unusual opportunity to experience the work of this little known and powerful composer.

—Thomas L. Noblitt
Indiana University

Limited Edition CD (1997)
40-page libretto in Latin, English, and German, ISBN 0-86516-346-4

Bolchazy-Carducci Publishers, Inc.
http://www.bolchazy.com